1899

Jayce

May your life unfold
with many treasures
and may all the love
you have shared be
returned to you many
times over
  May God Bless
      Phil Jordan

I Knew This Day Would Come

A Personal Journey to
Psychic Self-awareness

by

Phil Jordan
Psychic

Printed in the United States of America
First Printing: December 1998

ISBN: 0-9667537-0-4

To my friend, Dr. William Seaton,
you gave me the guidance and spiritual understanding needed
to embrace life

ACKNOWLEDGMENTS

Each person who has crossed my path has helped me write this book by what they have impressed upon my life. Special thanks to Kevin Sharp for his administrative skills and friendship and Georganne Gillette for her book design and editing expertise. My friend and mentor, Dr. Paddy Welles, has been an inspiration, with unconditional love and understanding. Ma and Dad, you did the best you knew how, without you there would be no story. To my sisters, Rose, Phyllis, and RuthAnn, and my brother, Rick, we can all look where we stand with wonderful pride. To the Thomas family, who adopted me as their own, may God bless you. To my friend, Bill, who never gave up waiting for the story I had to tell, thank you. To my friend, Ed, who gave me new insights, to my friend, Kay, for the years of laughter and encouragement. To Father David, who brought me to the right spiritual place. A special note of love to my forever friend, Corinne, I miss you, but I only have to look in my heart and memories and there you are.

FOREWORD

I sat on the front porch as a child and looked at the world, knowing I was different. I found it was that difference that made my world liveable. The gifts I have had entrusted to me weren't a curse but a code to survival. The things that only I could see were meant for me to see, perhaps to light a dark night or blaze a new trail. Although I sometimes feel alone in the presence of my gift, I know that I am not. They have brought me an abiding love in God and the company of thousands who have crossed my path. The memory of others may be different than mine, yet these are the pages of my life as I recall them.

Last night I sat at the cabin reminiscing. The cabin was the only place in my youth where I remember true peace and gentle love. I have kept my aunt and uncle's cabin as a haven of peace where I can retreat from the world and return to the past for the answers to life's questions. It is here where the pitcher pump and the outhouse connect generations. The birds still beckon the morning sun and the red skies promise a tomorrow. I watch the deer play in the new-mown fields as the road meanders beyond. The memories of yesterday making way for the gifts of tomorrow, just as they have forever.

I can still see the old Chevy with Ma at the wheel, winding its way up the road for a Sunday afternoon of good times. Ma was barely visible at the helm, the car so massive and Ma so short. My sisters shrouded in scarves to keep the dusty country road from violating their teenage beauty. My brother and I, carefree, mocking Ma's every driving skill.

I paused for a moment and wondered if the kids ever saw life the way I did. They must have. We all had hope and so many of our dreams have been answered. We all have a college education, beautiful homes, and wonderful people in our lives. The things that separated us in childhood have united us as adults. The atrocities of yesterday have become the family stories for the next generation. In the silence of my prayers I still ask God for the same things I did so many years ago: "Protect the ones I love, guide me to Your gifts, and help me to use them to Your satisfaction."

I suppose the kids never knew of my prayers all those years, or that they continue today. I know they knew of my struggle because they shared it with me. I don't know what they feel about my gifts, but I feel the love they have for me. They don't have to say anything because the gift of love is the strongest gift of all.

PREFACE

I guess I was always destined to survive. Although I often can't tell whether I am a success or a failure in whatever I do, I know the world is there with an opinion, so I have often left that up to them. I just know that I was fated to survive.

Through the years I listened as people talked of their scars through a lifetime of physical abuse. As I listen as sympathetically as possible, I want so badly to tell them that I would take a physical scar any day over the scars of emotional and psychological abuse that I endured. If I could touch a scar or see a sign of the years of tyranny I would know in my heart it was real. But, like so many of the secrets in my life, I have had to bury them in the dreams and nightmares of the past and trust that memory is the keeper of reality. I would love to silence the voice of the past that reminds me daily that I am a failure, that I can't succeed, that I am ugly and stupid, that I should have done the world a favor and killed myself, that I could never make anything of myself or meet anyone's expectations of me, not even my own.

Yet, when it comes to survival, the abuse from the past has become a battle cry. The challenge of making it from one day to the next in a life of poverty, dysfunction, and negativity has fueled the fires of passion for life. To succeed and become all I have been capable of becoming. To know that I was different in a special way and not a freak of nature, to know that I am unique and not weird, adequately intelligent and not simple has been a lifelong process.

Although I struggle to be at the top it isn't nearly as bad as the struggle it took to get there. I know that I am as vulnerable today as I was thirty years ago. Age and wisdom have been kind to me and, although I am not old, experience has been a good teacher.

I have watched myself come from having an instinct to survive, through an unconscious intuitiveness, to a wonderfully unique psychic awareness. To share that journey is to share my life. To open my heart is to receive the love the world has to offer me and to share the love I have to offer the world. As I reveal the secrets that have molded my life I know that I betray commitments to myself from the past, but I can no longer fight the battle without seeing the enemy. It is the battle that has stimulated the imagination, cultivated the intuitiveness, and pursued a psychic awareness, all in the name of survival.

Perhaps it is in sharing that another person will find hope. Hope that they too can survive. Hope that they will not be perceived as crazy or taunted into believing things about themselves that aren't true. Through this hope maybe they can find peace and comfort within themselves and come to know the nature of their own spirit and be strong enough to love themselves. I pray they will ascend from the pit of despair and loneliness to know that they are not alone, that they too can survive.

INTRODUCTION

I share the thoughts and stories of my life with you. I hope that they will help you understand your own spirit.

Your spirit is meant to be here at this time. Listen to that spirit as it walks through creation. Look at its weaknesses and create strengths from them. Look at its strengths and become humble. Never allow anyone, including yourself, to rob you of the spirit within your. Take time to love and nurture that spirit and be who God wants you to be. Learn to share in the love of your spirit and share your spirit in love.

Some of the things I share are wounds yet unhealed. Some are wounds that are healed but have left scars. Some are just wonderful memories that make my life what it is. I have come to understand the difference between love and hate. I have come to accept the difference in people and the role of human nature in the world in which we live. I have come to understand the presence of fear and the power of love. I know my faults although I often choose to deny them. I am still on my journey, seeking love and happiness. There have been people along that pathway that have been an integral part of that journey. Some have known of that love and some have denied it. Each day I pray that I can go through the day as honest as I allow myself to be. I pray through that honesty I can touch the true nature of the God within.

I do not expect life to always be a paradise but I am prepared to handle the most difficult moments and have discovered that life itself has taught me to do so. As a person whose life was marred by addiction and abuse, I have come to realize that we can rise above that or we can wallow in our own self-pity. I have recognized special gifts and talents within myself and have mingled those gifts with academic knowledge, spiritual belief, and an understanding of the human spirit so that each day, no matter what happens . . . , "I knew this day would come."

CHAPTER ONE

I was raised on dreams. My mother was intrigued by her dream life and was always interested in mine. She was aware that through her dreams she could understand herself and those around her through their dreams. She had an uncanny ability to interpret the dreams as they were revealed to her or another person. She would add a bit of intrigue and suspense with a bit of Irish folklore or superstition. If nothing else, it was most entertaining in my childhood to listen as dreams were told and interpreted.

For twenty-five years I have suggested that dreams become a part of therapeutic interest. A dream told of a person in their quest for knowledge will tell much more about them than they will tell about themselves. A dream is honest. It may be mixed with psychological happenings of the person as well as precognitive outcomes of that person's particular experience. Dreams may be simply a method of relaxation for an inquisitive mind. In understanding the dream world we will come to know ourselves. We will be able to interpret what is psychological, what may be physically induced, or what may be precognitive or psychic in nature.

Countless events in my life have involved dreams. A dream actually initiated my involvement into the field of psychic phenomenon.

I thoroughly enjoy my dream life and I dream four to six dreams each night. Some of the dreams I remember for the information that they may give me. Some I remember for the pleasures they bestow upon me, some may be so horrifying I choose to forget, and some may be insignificant dreams that are allowing mental relaxation to occur while my conscious mind is resting.

Many people have told me they do not dream. My first impulse is pity. I can't imagine a life without dreams. I have become aware that if I don't remember a dream I was either in such a deep state of sleep that it was recorded and placed in the unconscious mind without being noted by the conscious awareness or it was an insignificant dream that did not need to be remembered. It may have been something reserved for later use, or something I didn't need to remember at the time I dreamt it. People who believe they don't dream still dream, they just don't remember their dreams. The conscious mind seems to remember dreams that are essential to a person's life and well-being. We dream for self-preservation, sanity, and rest. The failure to remember dreams should not upset us but we should attempt to program our minds to remember dreams. Our curiosity wants us to become aware of what the mind is doing in sleep. Eventually, we can program ourselves not only to remember our dreams but to have dreams that are to our advantage, that benefit our spirit as we travel through life.

Many years ago I opened a small restaurant. In pursuing financing for the restaurant I applied for a loan at the local bank. My proposal for financial backing was rejected and I received a brief note from the loan officer. He said, "I cannot possibly finance a venture for something as risky as a restaurant but keep on dreaming, Phil."

I kept the note because I have kept on dreaming, while at sleep or awake. My dreams have taught me the strength needed to survive. They have created the goals for me to seek. My dreams have warned me and given me information necessary in my struggle to survive. To ignore my dreams, either conscious or unconscious, would be to reject the very spirit that dwells within my body.

Although I knew the banker had more of a personality conflict with me than a business conflict, I have taken his advice. A letter intended as a negative slap in the face became a missile of advice. I have kept on dreaming.

Frequently, I am asked when I first realized my psychic abilities. My response must be with an incident concerning a dream when I was sixteen years old. However, as I stop and think about my intuitive awareness, I reflect on several other incidences that occurred in my life at a much younger age. Until the dream at sixteen, I assumed that these feelings and intuitive experiences were all part of the human condition. I assumed everybody knew things ahead of time. Whether moments or months ahead, I thought everyone knew things that would affect their life before they got to those events. In my adult life I have found that not everyone has such awareness. I've discovered that we have a hesitancy in confronting things, of not wanting to deal with things, to deny the possibility of them becoming reality.

Many of my psychic experiences in life have been during sleep or just as I am going to sleep or coming out of sleep. This is when the mind is in its most natural state to receive impressions that might be psychic or precognitive in nature. Our unconscious awareness is equal to or greater than our conscious awareness. When we sleep our conscious mind rests. It rests because it's through the conscious mind that we continue to motivate our body, be aware of the world around us, and allow our life to fit into this world. We maintain an unconsciously alert mind in sleep. We not only have thoughts drifting in from the conscious mind but our unconscious mind still maintains an awareness of all the senses. It's the unconscious awareness that allows us to understand how we can consciously heighten our senses into an actual psychic awareness.

Our unconscious awareness in sleep may often perceive things in dreams that come to pass. Answers to problems which we may have worked on for a long time, such as the location of a lost item or the answer to a dilemma in our life. Our unconscious mind continues to perform in sleep and we create dreams that may give us the answers.

External stimuli may also create dreams. For instance, you may dream that you are at the scene of a fire or an accident, sirens are blaring and lights are flashing, when suddenly you awaken as a patrol car, an ambulance, or fire siren is blaring by your house. What happens is the external stimuli of the siren instantaneously creates a dream to accommodate itself.

There may be dreams where we feel an arm or a leg is severed and we awaken to find that the position of sleep on a limb has impaired circulation, giving a numbness or a sensation the limb was no longer attached to our body.

One evening in my early adult years I had a vivid dream that I was shot in the stomach. I could feel the burning sensation of the bullet radiating in one specific spot. The dream lingered with me for several days because of its horrifying nature. Three months later I was diagnosed with an ulcer in the exact spot where I felt the bullet had entered my body. My mind had perceived the ulcerative tissue before I physically felt it. Think of the consequences of extending that into reality, where the mind can perceive things about us physically and make us aware. How wonderful it would be to understand our dreams and thoughts psychically as a preventive measure with our health. Through this prevention we could maintain a quality of life as well as a quantity of life using the mind that God has given us.

To receive information psychically, we must transcend our conscious mind and become involved with our unconscious mind. The mind is basically broken into two categories: conscious and unconscious. Psychic perceptions are perceived through the unconscious mind. Human nature beckons us to stay in our conscious awareness, it's more comfortable. Through fear, more than anything else, we avoid the unconscious. We fear the loss of control. We think our conscious mind has control over what comes and goes in our life. If we attune to our unconscious mind we may confront things that go far beyond the scope of conscious awareness and human understanding. We bypass the conscious awareness of denial. Those things that bypass our conscious faculty prompt us to think that life is different than we perceive our reality to be. Early in life I generally would do anything to escape my conscious reality. I found it very easy to go into my unconscious mind. Daydreams were exciting. Meditative experiences were not only relaxing, but informative. Whether it was relaxing my body by counting from a hundred to one, a prayerful mediation involved in a church atmosphere, or merely saying prayers before I went to sleep, I found comfort, strength, and knowledge. Whatever the meditation, it allowed me to escape the realities of my world. I never thought myself mentally unhealthy, only that life was difficult. I needed to perceive how things would evolve or just get away for a respite from the uncertainties of my childhood. Nevertheless, in my unconscious awareness I would be mostly concerned with those I loved. They seemed to be all that I had in the world. My dreams would focus on their well-being, their happiness, their contentment in life.

Having a twin sister created a natural bond of conscious and unconscious awareness. I felt responsibility for someone other than myself. I was the extrovert, Phyllis was the introvert. I needed to protect her. I was aware when danger was near or if her life might be going toward the negative rather than the positive. Unconsciously through dreams and intuitive experiences I have always maintained a psychic and telepathic connection with my twin. I just *knew* what was happening in her life.

One warm summer afternoon, when I was about six years old, I was in my room taking a nap. As I awakened I had a vision that Phyllis ran across the front yard and fell on the knoll in front of our home. She stubbed her toe and fell spread-eagle in the cinders of the road. I got up and looked out the front window. Phyllis was running across the yard toward the road. I yelled at her but to no avail. I pounded on the window but in her excitement to catch up with friends she couldn't hear me. I watched as she flew across the cinders, cutting her lip, exactly as I had seen moments earlier.

Years later I had the distinct feeling that an uncle would die in January. I mentioned it to several people as I assumed others knew he would die then also. However, it was only August and people looked at me in a strange way.

In December our uncle's home caught fire. He was placed in a nursing home because of advancing dementia in his aging years and his inability to live alone. A month later, in January, he died.

Although I shed tears in grief, I couldn't fully understand why everyone was so upset over his death. After all, they knew of his impending death since August. They had a chance to make amends with him and do things for him. They could quiet their own guilt and regrets concerning his life. If they were upset they should have been upset with themselves. I was comfortable with myself. I knew ahead of time and had spiritually prepared myself not only for his death but the emotional consequences. I found that precognition (knowing ahead of time) helped to prepare me. It helped me to avoid worry and emotional conflict. Some people think it just gives you more to worry about or may even create a reality from imagination. For me it has always held an element of preparedness.

There is an interesting sidenote to my Uncle Bob's death. My twin sister and I went to his wake. It was the first time I had ever seen a deceased person. I couldn't believe how pale he looked in the casket. He truly looked dead. More amazing to me was the fact that the casket was lying down, like a bed. Movies I had watched on television, such as "Frankenstein" or "Dracula," showed the casket fully open and standing in a corner. I supposed, per chance, that if the deceased came back to life he could just step out of it.

As we walked into the funeral home that evening, straight ahead, through two rooms, was my uncle lying in the casket. I could see his large nose over the edge. I immediately knew it was my uncle because the large nose is a family trait recognizable to anyone. We stood looking at him as my mother, trying to ease the pain of the event, said, "Don't be so nervous, you're not going with him." I did become very anxious and nervous. I repeatedly asked, "Can we go now, can we go now, can we go now?" and Phyllis laughed. Ma said to us, "Why don't you two walk home."

It was a bitter cold evening as we approached the bridge that we had to cross on our way home. The winter winds seemed to pierce our flesh like needles. I suddenly felt danger. I knew we should run across the bridge. I said to Phyllis, "Let's run across this bridge, it's so cold."

The chill was really the feeling of danger that I had, so we ran across the bridge. Upon reaching the other side we heard a huge noise. An overloaded hay truck had gone too rapidly around the curve leading onto the bridge and overturned where we had walked a few moments before. Hay covered the road and sidewalk and bales were cast off into the creek. Phyllis and I looked at each other and ran for our lives. Our feet never stopped until we were safely in our living room warming our hands at the old coal stove. It was a fearful event, but one well remembered. Again, my feelings helped me to be safe.

I was a young man of sixteen in the spring of 1966 when I had a dream that would change my life. A dream so real that it was difficult to discern whether it was a dream or an actual life experience.

My Uncle Georgie was like a Dad to me. My own father, an alcoholic, was not available to be a father. Uncle Georgie (his real name was Leon) made himself accessible to me. He accompanied me to father-and-son banquets, bought baseball gloves, and tried to show a sense of fatherhood to a young man who was without a committed father.

I dreamt I was at my aunt and uncle's home. He stood in the living room, clutched his chest, and fell to the floor. My aunt called the ambulance.

He was taken to the hospital, diagnosed with a heart attack, and placed in a room tethered to all kinds of beeping and blinking machines, lapsing in and out of a coma. Although I was in the dream, it also felt like I was outside looking in, as if in a remote viewing.

The dream scenario continued at the hospital. My mother and I were in the emergency room looking for my uncle. We stood near two gray doors through which a nurse entered the room. I noticed her name tag as she informed us that my uncle was in very critical condition. It was doubtful he would survive. He would live another five hours, have another coronary, and, in his weakened condition, he would not survive. The doctors were giving him blood-thinning medications, oxygen, and everything possible to stabilize him but he was not responding. The nurse informed us that the doctor wanted to talk to us. Just then the doctor came through the gray doors. He repeated what the nurse had just told us. He patted me on the shoulder and said, "You're like a son to him, maybe if you were at his bedside it would be helpful to him. Why don't you go in and visit with him?"

I went into the room filled with specialized equipment. Georgie was sitting up in bed, smiling. He said to me, "They think I'm going to die but I'm not. I've got a long way to go yet. Don't worry, everything will be okay." He winked at me, laid back down, and went to sleep.

Then I woke up. I'm sure I had the dream shortly after going to sleep on that warm May night. It seemed an eternity before hours of darkness gave way to the dawn. There were so many thoughts I needed to share with someone. My mother, my main confessor, always had a good ear to listen. I knew she could interpret the meaning of my dream.

I told my mother of my troubled night's sleep at breakfast. I had just begun to tell her about the dream when I saw a neighbor coming across the yard to our front door. I instinctively knew what she was going to tell us. I said to Ma, "She is going to tell us that Georgie has had a heart attack."

My mother glanced a bit mysteriously at me as the neighbor shouted through the screen door, "Myrt, your sister Florence is calling. Leon has had a heart attack and is in critical condition at the hospital. She needs you to come to her immediately."

Ma didn't drive outside our community so she didn't know

how she would get to the hospital. I had received my learner's permit to drive only a few days earlier, so I drove us to the hospital twenty-five miles away. My biggest concern was whether our old '56 Chevy would make it.

On the way to the hospital I told Ma the details of the dream. We arrived at the hospital and hastily went to the emergency room. There we were greeted by a nurse, the same nurse that was in my dream. I watched my mother as she was told about my uncle's condition. It appeared my mother wasn't listening or comprehending what was being said to her. She was staring at the name tag on the nurse's uniform. The nurse completed her medical bulletin as the doctor came through the two gray doors. He told us of my uncle's worsening condition. He said, "This young man ought to go in and see him, it might cheer him on a bit."

They led me to my uncle's bedside. There, lying in the bed, attached to all kinds of equipment and cardiac-care apparatus, was the man that had been a father to me my entire life. The man who bought me my first baseball glove. The man who made sure I had a fishing pole. The man who opened his home to me during many summers so I could get away from the torments of an alcoholic home. The man I still needed in my life to go with me to father-and-son banquets. The only man I had loved as a father. Everybody was telling me that he was going to leave me. He was going to die.

I took his hand in mine and rubbed it in nervous hopefulness that he would wake up and be a healthy man. After a couple moments he turned his head and looked at me as if to find who was disturbing him. It took awhile for his eyes to focus. Medication was taking its toll on his consciousness. He saw it was me. He gave me the little crooked smile that was only his and winked at me. The same wink he had given me in the dream only hours before. He closed his eyes and went back to sleep.

My heart raced. I knew he was going to live. My constant and abiding prayers through the past few hours were being answered. The medical professionals and the family would all be wrong and my uncle would survive. I knew in my heart and no one would ever convince me differently.

One hour passed and he was still alive and showing signs of stability. Three hours, more stable. Five hours, the designated time for the death angel, greatly improved. Soon he was conscious and talking with us and we knew he was on the road to recovery.

He survived that near-fatal heart attack and lived thirteen more years. During that time he had three more heart attacks. Each time I knew as he became ill. I either called his home as the ambulance crew was attending him or arrived at his house while the squad was there.

On one occasion I was traveling in Florida and I suddenly knew that he had had another heart attack. I called home and my aunt briefly spoke to me as the medics were taking him from the house on a stretcher.

Another time, I was traveling to a lecture six hours away in the upper corner of New York state. Again, I knew he had been stricken with a heart attack. Sure enough, I called home and found that he had just been admitted to the hospital. The third time I was in a wedding and had just been served my dinner at the head table. Again, the feeling overpowered me. I excused myself and went to my uncle's house as they were loading him into the ambulance. Each time I knew and each time I wondered why I knew. In July of 1979, the day after my aunt and uncle celebrated their sixtieth wedding anniversary, he died.

Georgie had seemed tired at the party but so pleased to see all of his friends. We had a wonderful time. A friend of mine, a Franciscan friar, was visiting me. He had come to the party and stayed a couple days extra to visit. The next night I received a phone call at 1:00 a.m. It was my aunt, who said, "Your uncle is on his way to the hospital."

Brother Ray and I headed for the hospital. I told Brother Ray, "This will be the last time my uncle will go to the hospital. He will die within an hour after he's admitted."

We quietly discussed my feelings. When we arrived the staff assured us he was resting comfortably. They were about to transfer him to the intensive care unit. They suggested I be with my aunt.

I went to my aunt's house. Shortly after arriving the phone rang. I answered it. It was the hospital informing me that en route to intensive care my uncle had had another heart attack. He died shortly after I left the hospital. I was prepared. I was ready to let him go, thankful for the thirteen extra years I had shared with him. I could have been robbed of those years. I was prepared by the bond of love that was between us. The bond of love that told me each time that something was wrong with him. I knew that nothing, not even death, could break that bond.

Georgie had seen me grow from a fearful and insecure young man into a strong young man able to endure the pain of his death. I could make it on my own, he didn't need to protect me any longer. It was time for him to go and time for me to be on my way with my own life. And so together that night, in early July, we both let it be.

CHAPTER TWO

My first memory is that of Hurricane Hazel coming through the northeastern United States in October of 1954. I was four years old. I remember that we had taken my mother to the doctor. She had a severe case of sudden and unexpected rheumatoid arthritis. My aunt and uncle had taken us to the doctor and when we returned home the hurricane was beginning. The wind blew a beanie that my brother was wearing and we all chased after it across the road and down into a field. Finally, we caught the beanie and went into the house for safety, while my aunt and uncle continued to their home twenty miles away.

As the storm heightened in its intensity, Ma got the kerosene lamp from the cupboard and placed it in the middle of the buffet. Dad began to close the curtains, fearing breaking windows could injure one of us. As the winds worsened, we all huddled in the little bedroom occupied by my mother and sisters. Dad assured us everything would be all right.

Suddenly there was silence. The winds just quit. We listened intently as my father told us that it was the eye of the storm passing over. He said the winds would return and probably last the rest of the night—they did.

I remember looking at Dad and thinking how tall he was. I so wanted him to put his arms around me and embrace me like he did my sisters. I remember thinking how smart he was. After all, he knew all about hurricanes, something I'd never even heard of before that day. I knew if the house blew down we would still be safe in the arms of our mother and father. Although I also remember trembling with fear, I can recall the peace of knowing that safety.

If only life could have been that simple. If only I could have continued to walk in safety, trust, and confidence. As I look back on October of 1954 and Hurricane Hazel devastating parts of the northeast, I realize that is my first memory but it certainly wouldn't be my last storm. The storms of life often got much more severe than that hurricane. I would be tossed about and made to believe that I could no longer endure, yet something within kept me strong. Those enduring storms allowed me to believe . . . if only in myself.

Like every child I liked to hear stories about when I was born, childhood things that were insignificant to me but so significant to others. Things that I have forgotten, things I didn't know.

A story that seems to be commonly shared in my childhood, and even in my adulthood, is the story of my first introduction to alcohol. It was a week before I was born.

Dad was taking Ma to her doctor's appointment. She was so uncomfortable. The doctor wouldn't believe she was expecting twins and until the day we were born he insisted that it was one big baby boy. My mother jokingly told him she must be having an octopus because she could feel eight arms and legs. She *knew* she was having twins.

En route to the doctor's, Dad, not paying attention to his driving, got onto the shoulder of the road and the car went over a rather steep embankment. It seemed obvious it was going to roll over. Dad opened the door and ran alongside the car and held it upright so it wouldn't flip, causing injury to my mother and us unborn twins. The car came to a halt, held up by a young sapling. Dad reached under the driver's seat, removed all the whiskey bottles, and ran into the woods to hide them. He didn't want the investigation to reveal he had been drinking. That story is supposed to be humorous, yet forecasts such serious problems.

A week later, my twin sister, Phyllis, and I were born. The doctor entered the waiting room and told Dad that he had a baseball player, knowing Dad's affection for that game. Dad was elated. He ran off to call the boys back at the neighborhood pub. When he got back to the waiting room the doctor returned to tell him that he also had a cheerleader. Twenty minutes after my birth, my sister was born. I'm not sure who was more unsettled, my father who didn't expect it or the doctor who didn't believe it. It's no wonder my mother was so uncomfortable—Phyllis weighed seven pounds, two ounces and I weighed six pounds, fourteen ounces, and Ma was only four-foot-eleven inches. Before we were born she had to use a wheelchair because, when she stood up, she fell over frontwards.

My mother's sister, Aunt Florence, opened her home to my mother and us twins. She knew Ma wouldn't get the care at home that she needed. So our first six weeks of life were spent sleeping in a dresser drawer with a pillow in it as a crib. Rose, my older sister, was two at the time of our birth. She accepted me but didn't want Phyllis. It must have felt good to me to be accepted that early in my life because I never felt too accepted after that.

Three years after we were born, my little brother, Rick, came into the world, making the family complete, two girls and two boys. There we were, the family: Ma, Dad, and four children under the age of five.

Ma and Dad were in their early forties with four "change of life" babies, living in a two-bedroom house with an outhouse attached to the back, a pitcher pump in the kitchen, a wringer washer, no telephone, a home that had been purchased for $800. Ma had saved the money.

It would seem to have been a difficult situation to grow up in, but in all honesty I don't ever remember being hungry, being without shoes or clothing, and although I remember we lacked for a lot of things other kids had, we had enough to get along.

Dad worked factory jobs in our early childhood and although he was a weekend drinker, he always worked. He seldom even took the one week vacation that was offered during shutdown. If he did, he would take on a painting job so that we wouldn't lose a week's income.

Ma was busy with us kids and every other kid on the street. Most of the kids were left with babysitters as their Moms and Dads went off to work. Any kid that got into trouble, it was Myrt who saw them through. Trouble could be anything from taking them to the kerosene drum to get tar off their hands and feet after playing in the tarred road on a hot summer day or holding the neighbor girl while she had stitches after getting her hand caught in a wringer washer. The girl was trying to do the wash that her working mother asked her to do, even though she probably wasn't old enough.

Ma would teach us, nurture us, and nurse us the best way she knew how. I can still feel the pain of the mustard plaster she put on my back when I was sick. My whole back turned into one great big blister. I think the agony of the mustard plaster blister was much worse than whatever it was supposed to cure me of.

I had the whooping cough and chicken pox at the same time. I nearly strangled on the phlegm in my throat and lungs, so Ma placed a couple of drops of kerosene on a teaspoon of sugar and had me dissolve it in my mouth. I don't know whether it cut the phlegm or gagged me enough that the phlegm loosened, but it did. It's amazing it didn't kill me with chemical pneumonia, yet the two drops of kerosene on a teaspoon of sugar seemed so much better than sleeping in a small room with a creosote lamp. The lamp burned with a small flame, filling the room with acrid smoke. It forced the croup out of my body by causing me to cough continuously.

Growing up, I knew we were poor people but I knew we were good people. We knew right from wrong because we were taught by people who knew right from wrong. Our faith was simple and natural. We tried to be good in a bad place in life and no matter how difficult times got we always had each other. That seems to be the peace I felt in my early life until it began to change. Dad's drinking worsened, Ma's health got poorer, and the struggles seemed to intensify. Peace, safety, happiness, and that idyllic childlike innocence of youth disappeared. It disappeared about the same time Dad decided I'd be a baseball player. It was about the same time I decided I hated baseball.

CHAPTER THREE

It would be difficult to look at one's life without observing the influences of the people around you, especially your parents. A Dalmatian's spots don't come from strangers. I've had a very strong influence of both parents in my life. Some aspects are wonderful, while some are not so good. All in all, the early experience of my childhood and adolescence was greatly and dramatically shaped by the attitudes of my Mom and Dad.

Dad was truly a great man. After all, every child wants to be able to say that about his father. Unfortunately, during the part of my life when my Dad was significant, I never realized it. It's been in the years since his death, and truly in very recent years, that I've understood the good side of my father and how much of me is part of him.

I remember Ma saying, "Death does not make saints out of bastards." In the years since my father's death I have come to understand him. I am able to look at him in a positive perspective, not forgetting the bad but honoring the good. Time has allowed me to separate the wheat from the chaff and know my father was a good person. It was several years after his death before I realized that I had a love for him and that he had a love for me. Thank God I've come to realize that love. It has made the years since a lot easier.

I now live in the present with hopeful anticipation of the future rather than in a past life of abuse and misery. It's good to know from whence we came so that we'll be on guard not to go back there.

Dad came from poor people. There were seven children in his family. His mother died when he was sixteen years old. The family split apart because of her death, journeyed to different foster homes or to older sisters who raised younger brothers and sisters. Some, such as my Dad, tried to fend for themselves.

His father was a slow-moving, slow-talking, not overly ambitious man. Granddad was a kind person, but never accepted more responsibilities than the day would allow, especially those of a family with young children. He was a hired man for area farmers who worked enough to keep himself in chewing tobacco, food, and a roof over his head. Other than that he never expected a lot more out of life.

Dad, on the other hand, was an eager young man, full of energy. He wanted to do things with his life and had an excitement within that was very hard to squelch. He lived for the moment, which gave way to drinking at an early age, and he continued to drink heavily throughout his life.

His sidekick was his younger brother, Howard. They called him Ikie. They had the bond of brothers, but a stronger bond as friends. They shared life together and enjoyed it. Big brother looked after little brother and vice versa.

The call came to serve the country in World War II. Those who were not drafted enlisted. Dad was in his mid-thirties, his brother in his late twenties. They both enlisted in the Army and before long found themselves off to war.

Howard had married and fathered a baby girl. Dad was still single with lots of girlfriends.

I wasn't born until 1950, yet I lived and relived World War II throughout my childhood. I knew most of the battles that my father fought in and came to realize at a very early age that those battles continued long after the war ended.

Dad saw terrible times during World War II, as many of the GIs did. The trauma of war changed him into a man who felt that he had to battle the rest of his life. He had to fight the good fight. He had to be a patriot. Most of all, he had to be a man. The war killed his sensitivity to the world around him. He went into himself and was never again to share his life as fully as he wanted. It's an unfair and unjust tragedy of war that we perpetuate time and again.

In the spring of 1944, Dad was shipped to England. His battalion was waiting for involvement in the European Theater. He was stationed in England, waiting to be shipped into Normandy. According to the stories I heard as a child and throughout my life, Dad was in a smoke-filled pub in England, having a few beers the night before he was to ship out, standing at one end of the bar, when he looked to the other end and saw his brother whom he hadn't seen for months. They spent a wonderful evening together reminiscing, sharing in the good times of their lives as well as the fears and uncertainties that waited in Europe.

Dad, having fended for himself, was a survivor, and although he looked with doubt at his future, there was a certainty that he knew would see him through. I can't forget that quality about him. No matter how difficult times got, he would always brace himself with the assurance that he could succeed, that he would make it somehow.

It was revealed later that Howard had a lot of uncertainty. Before shipping off to war he had given away many of his personal possessions. He gave his fishing boots to a friend and told him that he wouldn't be needing them any more. That evening, in that smoke-filled pub in England, must have been like a Humphrey Bogart movie, filled with excitement, emotion, and melancholy.

Dad shipped out the next day and was on the fifth wave at Omaha Beach. Normandy and Omaha Beach was one of the bloodiest battles of the war. I fought that battle with Dad and his memory at an early age. I listened to him as he would tell that his feet never touched sand for the first mile up the beach, that he struggled to make his way up the beach walking over body after body after body. He prayed that he would get another mile and then another mile under the artillery fire of the front-line enemy. His only instinct was to survive. Somehow, he did.

He made it through that D-Day invasion and continued to stay alive throughout the rest of the war. His brother wasn't so lucky.

In August of 1944 Howard had made it to France. He was on reconnaissance duty and story has it that he came across a wounded soldier and helped him to a first-aid station. He realized that in the excitement he had left his gun back where he had found the soldier. Of course, a soldier can't be separated from his gun, so he immediately went back for the rifle. As he retrieved his weapon he was ambushed. He died there, leaving behind a wife and a three-month-old baby and his best friend, my father.

My middle name is Howard, named for my uncle. I've always tried to carry the name with pride. I have often thought how much I would love to have known him as he was such a part of my father's memories.

Dad continued with the war, heading toward Germany. He was a sergeant in the signal corp. His duty was to string communication wire from one post to another. At one point they were stringing wire across a river on a pontoon bridge and six of the eight men under him were in a boat stringing wire along the bridge. An artillery shell hit the boat and killed all six men. Dad, being the sergeant, had to write home to the families and explain what had happened, another source of the many nightmares that haunted him for a lifetime.

The war was coming to an end and things seemed hopeful. Dad made it to his destination in Germany. Many times he was busted from rank of sergeant for drinking. The commanding officer would commend him as a good soldier, but chastise him for drinking. Each time Dad was busted, within weeks he was reinstated to the rank of sergeant.

There were other hazards besides the war that he often talked about. He met a woman in Germany and fell deeply in love with her in a matter of a few minutes. In the course of the evening things advanced and as they became more intimate the woman pulled a knife and tried to stab him to death. He often tells how he immediately lost any affection for her in that random act of violence.

The war ended and Dad was shipped home, back to Fort Dix, New Jersey. He would muster out of Fort Dix to come home to family and friends.

He had received letters from home and was anxious to get there. He knew his father was advancing in age and that his health was failing. Dad couldn't wait to see him, his brothers and sisters, and all the friends who had written him during the war.

After he was released from Fort Dix, he got on a bus and headed for home. It was a long ride with lots of time to think. When he got home he stood in front of the neighborhood bar, probably the last place he had been before the war. He went into the pub to gather news and to see his special friend, Marie. She had written to him throughout the war. She met him with a fond embrace. She knew he had no knowledge of what had happened, that he had to be at his father's funeral within the hour. She told him they had tried to page him at Fort Dix but were told that in the confusion and frustration of so many GIs mustering out, he probably didn't hear the page, which he didn't. He went to his father's funeral realizing that life had been unkind once again.

I miss the stories that Dad told, especially after he had had a few drinks. They brought to life all the people that had died. He could tell a story better than anyone I knew. It was fun just to sit and listen.

Often Dad would toot his own horn and tell how he could have been the best baseball player in the whole country if only he hadn't drank. He was scheduled for tryouts with a farm team for the major leagues. He got drunk that day and never made tryouts. His regrets were forever, and, according to his friends, he probably *could* have been a professional.

I guess that's why I was supposed to be a baseball player. I guess that's why I was supposed to have been everything he wanted me to be. Unfortunately, life didn't go that way. I've always wondered if our relationship soured at an early stage because I was named for his brother who was killed in France, or because I had no interest in baseball and no physical size to accomplish any sport, or just that I was so independent. The only thing I know is that the relationship did sour. The more he tried to channel me in one direction, the more I wanted to go into another. I didn't want to end up like him, I didn't want to end up being drunk and irresponsible. So as life went on I pretty much did the opposite of what I knew he wanted me to do. I guess I thought if I did the opposite, I would turn out okay. He thought that if I would do what he told me to, I would be a man. He had a real fear that I wouldn't be a man. I had too many interests that were not of "manly quality." I liked church. I found comfort and peace in church at an early age, serving as an altar boy and being in the choir. I loved music. I liked the beauty that God had to offer us in flowers. I enjoyed things that weren't masculine. Dad began to call me a sissy. He said I would never amount to anything. He lived with the hope that I would change but knew I never would.

Dad never punished me physically. He never whipped me once. He always left that up to my mother even though occasionally he would donate his black leather belt for that purpose. The only one of us he ever laid a hand to was my brother, Rick. One day he was playing on Dad's lap, reached up and bit Dad on the nose. I think the shock of the whole thing was what fueled the fire that took Rick to the woodshed and convinced him he shouldn't be doing such things.

The memory that haunts me the most about my relationship with Dad, besides the constant pecking at me about being a man, was during my eleventh year. Two separate incidents made me realize that I could never please my father, that I could never become the man that he wanted me to become, and that his love for me was just not evident.

During the summer of that year, an incident occurred at the Little League field on the Fourth of July. I would never participate or enjoy sporting events again.

I had decided in late winter that I would do my very best to play baseball for one reason alone—to please my father. I had no interest in baseball whatsoever and didn't care for the competitive nature of any sport. I felt to succeed should be an individual thing and not a team effort and that while I might be able to contribute, success had to be my own.

Nevertheless, I registered for Little League. I got my uniform and waited for Dad to buy me a baseball glove. I waited and waited and waited. Then one Saturday he finally took off to buy my glove. He came home with an old tattered glove that somebody had given him. He used the money Ma had given him for my glove and got drunk instead. As I looked at the glove, I knew that I couldn't use it, let alone face the embarrassment of having to take it to the ball diamond. I cried for the rest of the day.

A few days later, my Uncle Georgie came with a brand-new baseball glove and in the web of the glove he had placed my name in green letters. At last, "the Babe" could step up to the plate.

It became apparent early that spring that a baseball player I was not. Yet I was on a team where there were a lot of good players and we did well. I was satisfied that I never got to play. When I did, it was way out in right field where people could barely identify me. Eleven-year-olds very seldom hit a ball out there. When they did, it was sheer horror for me. I would throw the ball in an endeavor to get it to the second or first baseman, but I could never get it to them. I was too small and too weak and just not able to wing a ball that far.

Our team won that year and we were placed as the All Star team in the big game of the year during the town's July Fourth celebration. I literally became sick thinking about having to play in front of what seemed thousands of people. Fourth of July was a big event. I now know that what seemed to be thousands of people were probably a hundred and fifty people, it just seemed like thousands. I had graduated from right field to second base, only because the second baseman was out of town with his family on vacation. His parents wouldn't change their vacation plans for his All Star game so I had to play second base, which made me extremely nervous.

Back in those days there was a rule that people could only pitch so many hours each week. Each child, once their amount of time in pitching was accomplished, was not allowed to pitch any-more. Dad stood at the sideline cheering me on. I remember stand-ing on second base with that wonderful feeling that at last I was pleasing my father. At last I could be the man that he wanted me to be. I thought, "Maybe this is just the start of the major leagues for me. I could go on with the New York Yankees and do everything that he didn't do."

The game was going great. It was a close game I remember, although I don't remember the score.

Suddenly we took a time out and I could see the coach walking toward me. My first thought was that I had done something wrong. Maybe I had broken a rule playing second base as I knew nothing about it. Then, as he walked closer, I instinctively knew that he was going to ask me to pitch. How could I tell him no? "I will just say no," I said to myself.

He came out and put his hand on my shoulder and said, "Phil, all the pitchers we have are over their time limit and you're the only one left. We're going to have you pitch for the next two innings."

If only second base could have opened and swallowed me up, but it didn't.

I said to him, "But, Coach, I've never pitched before. I don't know anything about it and I don't want to do it."

"You don't have any choice. You have to do it."

The crowd went crazy as I went to the pitcher's mound, one side knowing that they now stood a wonderful chance of winning, the other side cheering and booing in unison, a mockery of what they were about to see.

I looked to the left field line and there stood Dad. He was drunk, in his usual Fourth of July condition. He was throwing his fists in the air, saying, "Go get 'em." Although that was the encouragement I had sought for years, it wasn't what I needed at that time. I wanted so bad for him to come out on the field, meet me halfway, embrace me, pick me up and carry me off the field. I wanted to go home, never to see that ball diamond again. He didn't. He stood there and cheered and yelled to me to do the best I could—"Strike 'em out."

I got the ball in my hand and wound up for the pitch in a way that I had only seen done before but had never done. I finally released the ball toward home plate. Thump—thump—thump. Three times it bounced before it rolled over home plate. The crowd went wild. I retrieved the ball and wound up, visualizing in my head the best pitchers I had ever seen on television, in school, or anywhere. I tried to imitate and become one of them, if only for that two innings. I released the ball. Thump—thump—thump—thump. Again, my strength would not allow the ball to remain in the air long enough to be in the strike zone or anywhere near where the batter could hit it. It was that second ball when Dad began to yell at me. "You're worthless," he screamed between each pitch, abusing me and trying to invite me to get one across home plate. Finally I got one across. It was high and outside. Ball. The third ball. Again I released the pitch. Ball four. The batter walked to first base. The coach came out and told me, "Throw it a little higher, a little harder." Every ounce of muscle I had, every bit of power I could muster, I put into that ball.

The game became more and more a charade of a young man who would have given his soul to the devil to be a baseball player at that moment. Dad was yelling louder and louder and people were looking at him as he shouted, "You dumb fucking son-of-a-bitch, can't you throw a ball?" I wanted to throw my glove down and say, "Why didn't you teach me? Why didn't you toss balls back and forth with me? Why didn't you give me some of your talent? Why did you have to stay out drinking all the time and not be a father to me? Why? Why? Why?"

The game ended and we lost. I walked off the field, never to return.

The game proved to be the beginning of the end of our relationship as father and son. I stayed away from him for weeks on end and he, in his own way, avoided me. Occasionally, when he would get drunk and I'd be home, he would taunt me with being a sissy and being simple-minded, telling me, "You are a simple-minded son-of-a-bitch, aren't you."

It was then that I vowed to myself that I would go on and do everything I could with my mind. I would prove to him that I could be a man in other ways besides on a baseball field. I would have a mind that would supersede any other minds. If only he would be patient, I would prove to him that I could be a son.

On Christmas Eve of that year I was dressed in my suit and tie, waiting to go to Midnight Mass. It was my favorite time of year. It always seemed like church on Christmas Eve was like going to heaven with all the candles and flowers and the choir singing, and I was a part of it. I was an altar boy and they depended on me and needed me. For days before Christmas Eve I would remember the year before and how beautiful it was and imagine how this year would be even more beautiful.

Dad had come home from the bar drunk, and had fallen asleep in his chair while I sat on the sofa watching television. I could tell from his ramblings as he talked in his sleep that he was dreaming that I was doing something wrong and he was going to punish me for it.

Suddenly he aroused from his sleep and stood up. As if still in that dream, he grabbed me by the collar and pulled me off the couch. Ma ran in from the kitchen, separated the two of us, and asked him what was wrong with him. He raised his finger to my face and told me, "The only thing that I want to see before I die is you in a casket." It was unbearable to think my own father would say such a thing at any time of the year, but especially on Christmas Eve.

I remember, in detail, everything about that night. Where the tree was. Where Ma stood. Where he stood. What they were wearing. I knew I had to leave the room or things would get more intense so I ran up to my bedroom. I laid on my bed and cried into my pillow until my eyes swelled shut. I'm sure I didn't look very good for Midnight Mass, but I vowed he wasn't going to rob me of that special night. I brushed myself off and headed to the church. It was that night I asked God to protect me from my father, the person that was supposed to protect *me*.

The whole scene seemed to launch my need for independence. Even though I was young, I knew I could make it on my own. The following year, at the age of twelve, I got my first job as a paper boy. I had already helped on a paper route, but this one was my very own. It helped to create in me a discipline and gave me some sense of financial security with a few dollars in my pocket each week. Even at that early age, I realized the importance of having money to do what you wanted to do. However, in many alcoholic homes, it seems that the more the wife and children bring in, the more the alcoholic spends. Many times my money went to keep the household going. If I didn't give it to my mother she would seek out the place where I hid it and help herself. When I got home from school she would tell me that she needed it to pay a bill or keep groceries in the house.

At the age of fourteen I got working papers and was able to secure a job at a corner grocery store. This, again, gave me the sense of security that I needed.

Dad's drinking seemed to worsen from a few weekends a month to every weekend and even sometimes certain nights of the week. Previously, he would never go to work drunk, but now he was beginning to see the need for a drink to brace himself for the day ahead or calm himself after that day's work was done.

Many times I begged my mother to leave him. "Take us four

kids and get an apartment. We can make it and most of all we would be happy."

In her co-dependent mind she still held onto the hope that he would straighten his life out and we would become the happy family, stamped with the "Good Housekeeping Seal of Approval."

One very hot summer night, my mother and I sat on the front porch and I heard my sister get out of bed and go into the bathroom. I could hear her vomiting. Somehow I knew she was pregnant. I said to my mother, "Rosie is in the bathroom throwing up and I don't think she's sick. I think she's pregnant."

I didn't even know that much about pregnancy and what it did to the human body, but I knew she was pregnant and I knew that times were about to get more difficult. Ma confronted Rose. Sure enough, she was expecting. The fireworks began when she had to tell my father. He blamed my mother for the entire mess. He assured her that if she had not been a tramp and a whore that her daughter would not be pregnant. He accused Ma of everything from having affairs with the neighbors to going uptown and selling herself. I laugh when I think of it. My mother was short and fat, nothing attractive, and never left home. He knew that was a button he could push to get a fight started so that he would have a reason to go out drinking. He often pushed that button. Then he would come home and elaborate on the fight that he had started five hours earlier.

As for Rose, little did either of our parents know that she would do well for herself with her own instinct to survive. Although she left high school in her sophomore year to have the baby, she went back and graduated as president of her class, continuing on to receive a four-year college degree.

Living under the constant tension and anxiety of never knowing when a fight would erupt, I prayed that he would leave the house to go drink and be gone for most of the day. I became fearful about his return. It made me very aware of his presence at all times, whether he was physically present or not.

I would often stand in the window where I could see down the street. A few moments before he would return, I would intuitively know and would broadcast a warning to everyone in the house so that we could all assume our places. We could hide or go to our rooms. Ma would be doing something so that she wouldn't be accused of being a lazy, rotten, no-good bitch. This practice helped me considerably with telepathy. Even if he was gone eight hours I could sense his return within minutes before it actually occurred.

One Saturday afternoon I had just come home from doing my newspaper collections. I was resting for a few moments before I went to work at the store when Dad pulled in the driveway (the old Chevy made such a noise that it would have awakened the dead), and it certainly alerted me, although I slept with one eye open anyway.

Dad came into the house. He was drunk. He immediately provoked a fight with my mother. She was in the kitchen and he was in the living room. The small dining room was between them. Dad would often drink Peppermint Schnapps to get drunk faster. There was something about the high-sugar content that made him very ugly. It was obvious from the smell of peppermint that he had been in the Schnapps that day.

He and my mother proceeded to argue for, probably, a half hour to an hour. I was trying to sleep on the sofa. Suddenly I heard my mother scream. I ran to the kitchen as the tone of the scream told me that he was hurting her. Dad had never become physical with his violence, although it was often threatened. This was one time he not only threatened but proceeded to twist her arms behind her back and pull her hair. I've never felt such immediate rage in my entire life. Such a blinding rage that insanity tends to take over when somebody is hurting the one you love. I became so angry that I didn't know what I was doing.

I ran to the gun rack and grabbed the shotgun Dad used for deer hunting. I grabbed some shells and tried to get them in the gun. They didn't fit. I ran to the kitchen with the empty gun and held it on him until he let Ma go. He backed down immediately. He was sure that it was loaded and he knew that I was insane with rage. I screamed at him with tears running down my face and off my chin. I told him to get out. Just get out. I began to shake. My knees weakened. I wasn't sure what he was going to do next. I remembered that he had taught my sister Rose how to load and use a gun but he never taught me. It was probably a good thing.

I put the gun down and he pushed me up against the wall. He told me to never point a gun at anyone unless I intended to use it. I looked him in the eye and said, "I had every intention of using it, I just didn't get the right shells."

He walked away. I ran to the cellar and sat on the bottom step and cried from all the pain I had gathered through the years. I opened my pocketknife and carved on the back of the cellar door, "I hate life" and signed it "Phil." I've often wondered if those words are still there, a testament to some of the horror of a boy, trying to become a man, without the guidance of a father. From that day on Dad seemed to have a different attitude toward me, even a bit of respect.

When I was about ten Dad decided that he was going to teach me to drive. He instructed me to back the car out of the driveway, but never explained to me about the clutch, the brake, or the gas pedal. He just told me I had to use them. I was moving in reverse out the driveway faster and faster when I backed into a tree and knocked the bumper up on the back of the car. I jumped out of the car and almost fainted from the fear of what I had done. He apparently thought that I was trying to kill all of us and decided that I probably shouldn't learn to drive right away.

A bit later, I learned to drive. It was an ordeal in itself. Ma tried to teach me as Dad wouldn't because I was "too stupid." Ma was four foot eleven and looked through the steering wheel to drive. She became fearful at any speed over ten miles an hour. I was a young man who needed to go a bit faster than that.

Fortunately, I was older than the other kids in my class. I enrolled in driver's education and that's where I really learned to drive. Shortly after I got my driver's license I had saved enough money to buy my own car. Of course, it couldn't be a car I wanted, it had to be a car that Dad found for me. Mechanics was not one of Dad's areas of expertise. He had gone to a local jip joint and had become convinced that this 1961 Falcon would be the perfect car for me. It had no back springs and any time I went across a railroad track or hit a slight bump it would bounce for the next half mile. Sort of a fun car, but certainly not the car of my dreams.

We got the car home and it wouldn't start. Of course I was stupid again. It was my money that was spent and not his, so it was okay. My car became the second car for the family so if his car wasn't working he would use mine. Mine usually had gas in it. He registered and licensed it in his name which permitted him to feel perfectly fine in using it. I was able to use my car on some occasions. It got good mileage and provided a lot of fun times.

During my second semester of college my car died. Early one week I called home to see if I could use the family car that weekend to visit my roommate and his friends who wanted me to meet them at his home thirty miles away. That Tuesday night when I called, Ma assured me everything would be okay. "You can use the car on Friday night so make your plans."

I arrived home Friday afternoon and began to get ready for my trip. I asked for the keys and Ma said, "Dad has them in his pocket."

I asked him for the keys and he said, "You're not using the car tonight. Your brother wants it."

"You know, I asked you Tuesday night if I could use it. I have friends that I want to meet."

He replied, "I know what you asked Tuesday night but tonight is Friday night and I'm letting your brother use the car." He gave the keys to my brother who immediately left. I was so angry I went to the local pub and paid a man to drive me halfway to my roommate's house. This was a man who was on the edge of insanity all of his life. I risked my life that night riding with him, yet I didn't feel it was worth a hell of a lot at that point, anyway.

I walked the additional seven miles in sub-zero weather and was three hours late. I never did meet the friends or find my roommate. I was so hurt and angry I could have walked fifty miles that night. It gave me a lot of time to think about my life and where it was headed. It wasn't good. I knew my life had become totally focused on negativity. It was impossible for me to find any happiness or contentment. I relived all the horrifying experiences of a child of an alcoholic. I prayed that things could be better and realized they probably would not be. It became apparent to me that if I was going to survive, I would have to do it on my own or decide not to. It was that simple.

Through the years I watched as my father was apprehended repeatedly by the police for drunk driving. Each time they would release him without charges. He was in life-threatening accidents but he always escaped.

One Fourth of July afternoon Dad ran over a man at the town's

Fourth of July celebration. The cops brought Dad home again, only this time he went to court. The man had been injured and he filed a lawsuit for civil proceedings against my father. I prayed that Dad would lose his license. Life would be better if he couldn't drive to get the booze. He retained a local attorney and they proceeded to court, only to find out that the judge had thrown the case out. There was no proof as to whether Dad was drunk and hit the man or if the man was so drunk he walked into my father and was injured. There was no need for a trial. Once again, Dad was set free.

It's interesting that you can listen to people and know exactly what has happened. Every time Dad came home and said to my mother, "Well, Myrt, I've done it again," we immediately knew that he had wrecked another vehicle or he had been pulled over by the police.

I can still hear the promises to himself being echoed from the living room chair, "That's it. I'm never going to drink again. Once I get through with this one, I'm done. I'm never going to drink again."

He never drank again until that night or the next day. Quite simply, it was a life of terror. Even through all that terror, I prayed for my father. I knew of the hurt in his life and would imagine the drink soothing the pain. The pain of being orphaned at an early age, the pain of the war, the loss of a brother, the loss of his father, the hard luck that constantly beset him. I did not realize that a lot of that hard luck he had created for himself.

I prayed that I could be a better son, but about the only thing I could see my prayer doing was strengthening my faith. Nothing seemed to be getting answered, yet I knew that God was there. I knew that He listened. I was able to retreat by going to college, to physically separate myself from the terror. The constant phone calls from Ma telling me what Dad had done that day kept it ever-present. It haunted me. Even though I was physically away from it, I knew that she had to live in it.

College was a very difficult time. I had to take care of myself, not that I hadn't before, but I had to do that among strangers. I still had to keep things okay at home. I needed to protect my mother and try to bring some income to her. Yet every cent was needed for school. I traveled home each weekend to work in the local grocery store and tend bar part-time. I hated tending bar because I had to deal with people that were just like my father. I didn't ever want to be like my father.

I began to see that, if I could have a few drinks, my life seemed more comfortable, or at least the uncomfortable parts didn't matter. I began to drink rather heavily. I hated myself for it. I did things that seemed beyond me as a person. They seemed against my grain from a spiritual standpoint. In one aspect my spirit was growing and becoming beautiful while in another aspect it was being eroded by a disease that I had lived with my entire life. I was in a spiritual tug-of-war. One minute believing in myself and my right to survive and the next minute knowing that I was destroying myself. I was headed toward the destination that my father had predicted for me so many years before. I was headed toward the failure and unbearable misery that he knew was waiting for me. I could hardly bare it. My mind was constantly thinking of how I wanted to live or *if* I wanted to live. It seemed as if all the goals I had anticipated became fantasies, unobtainable fantasies. It was hard to study and most difficult to live. It was then that I decided I had to make the decision on whether I wanted to live or die.

CHAPTER FOUR

It was long ago but I remember it as if it were last night. It was a late October night, the fullness of fall was making way to the coldness of winter. The rain was more of a mist as I made my way to St. Mary's Church.

As I approached the steps going up to the main doors of the church, the bells tolled the eleventh hour. I had tried the door earlier on my way home from classes and found that it had been left open. I guess, even in a city, the church still has faith that people will come in to pray and find a new path in life. Apparently the element of trust is still an integral part of faith or perhaps they just simply forgot to lock the door.

I pressed the massive door open and proceeded into the foyer of the church. I immersed my fingers in the holy water by the door and blessed myself as I entered the sanctuary. My feet squeaked on the marble floor as I proceeded down the main aisle to the knave of the church. It was dimly lit from the flickering altar light and the votive candles that lighted peoples' prayers to heaven.

I knelt at the altar rail, clutching a rosary that a Catholic friend had given me, mumbling the Hail Marys and offering Our Fathers, seeking any consolation that I could find. Everything seemed perfect. It was the eleventh hour and I was alone except for the statues. They seemed almost lifelike. The opportunity had arrived to accomplish the task that my aching heart told me I must do.

In my pocket, folded inside a wad of cotton taken from an aspirin bottle, was a double-edge razor blade. I found it rather amusing that I was worried about cutting myself and had painstakingly wrapped it in cotton and Saran Wrap to transport it to the church.

I got up from prayer and walked from statue to statue, from station of the cross to station of the cross, talking to the stone statues as if they could hear. Per chance, they could come down from their pedestals just for a moment and hold me in their arms and let me sob. Maybe they would understand how much I hated myself. Life's events had led me to this act of insanity and perhaps one of the outstretched hands would grab my hand, embrace my shoulders, and give me the strength that I needed to live on.

I continued to talk, to pray, to listen. I confronted my first twenty years as I rambled on about the abusiveness of living in an alcoholic home and a father who hated me. The father who only months before begged me to quit high school and go into the military. "Oh, God, why didn't you take me to Vietnam so I could be killed as a soldier and die as a man?" I could stick a gun in my mouth and blow my head off my shoulders and do the world a favor, just like Dad wanted. I could please him. Ah, the echoes of the past in that stone church. Echoing a fight for survival. Echoing what alcohol and poverty had done. There had to be a better world than this, the church promised me that.

I was Episcopalian and I knew the church condemned murder of any kind. The self-inflicted death that I intended certainly would not allow me a church funeral. Even in my insanity my faith was strong and the importance of the church was profound. So, in this chaos, I decided that if I couldn't have a church funeral I would die in a church. I would be taken from the church for burial. I knew God would embrace me more quickly or perhaps understand my suicide more readily if I accomplished it in a church.

My hands were shaking as I took the plastic bundle from my pocket. I peeled away the Saran Wrap and opened the cotton to reveal the double-edge razor blade. I was careful not to cut my fingers. How crazy must I be? I hated pain but the pain of living seemed worse than the pain of the moment. I knelt and looked at the statue of the Blessed Mother, at the outstretched arms of Christ on the cross, and then at my wrist.

I begun to make the incision when suddenly the back door of the church opened. I heard footsteps walking briskly up the aisle. "Oh my God, somebody has caught me," I thought. Hastily I returned the razor to its cotton sheath and wrapped the Saran Wrap around it. I held it in my clenched fist. The steps came closer. I had convinced myself it was a nun or a priest coming to check the church. I caught a glimpse out of the corner of my eye of a very short person. I heard quickened breathing, punctuated by sobs. I looked to my right as a short woman, in a long gray tweed coat with a scarf around her head tied tightly under her chin, knelt at the altar. She reminded me of my mother. She was short and fat like my mother. She wore her scarf a lot like my mother. It made a visor over her face but even that couldn't hide the sweet innocence of her face.

Tears were streaming down her cheeks. She was dabbing the water that was coming off the end of her nose. It was obvious she had suffered a great loss.

I went to her and knelt beside her and simply said, "What's

the matter?" She said, "I don't want to live any more." In her thick Polish accent she continued, "I just left the hospital. My husband of sixty-two years just died and I want to go with him. I want to die, too. I do not want to be alone. I need to be with him."

I put my arm around her and embraced her. I responded, "But if God wanted you to be with your husband, you would have died together. You would have died in an accident or in a fire. But God didn't want you tonight. He wanted your husband. You still have things to do. You must stay here. You must be here. It won't seem very long before you'll be with your husband. So stay and do the things God is asking you to do now."

As my final words to her echoed in my head, I heard what God was telling me. I sensed a peace come through the top of my head. The bitterness that was destroying my soul seemed to be leaving through my feet. The desire to die had left me. The recognition of my being began to enlighten my soul and I found peace.

I've often thought of that wet October night so many years ago when a tortured young man, no longer wanting to be in this world, hating every moment and each breath that was taken, wandered into that church that just happened to be open. I knelt and prayed and talked to God and to the statues. I prayed for peace to my troubled soul and an act of God, the death of an old man, sent his wife to that church at precisely the right moment.

I never knew her name and never saw her again, except for all the times that face has appeared before me as an angel of mercy who changed my life. She let me know that through the power of God I'm never alone.

There are different times in our lives that we feel the need to know the presence of God in our life and then other times we just know that He is there.

I remember as a child being in my dark bedroom at night. We had no electricity or heat in our bedrooms, so I hid under the covers to say my prayers. I was fearful that I would forget somebody and they would go through some awful fate just because I had forgotten them. I knew Jesus stood right by my bed and protected me. He listened to my prayers and then took them to God in the night. My prayers became quite involved and it was through those early days of prayer that I found God.

A year later I began my third year of college at Brockport State Teacher's College. Thanksgiving break had arrived. It's such a busy time and transportation home was near impossible. A friend of mine offered me a ride home with her and her family. I had a final exam but she thought that would be no problem as it would be only a fifty minutes' wait longer than they anticipated. They could grab a piece of pie and some coffee and wait for me and then we would be on our way.

She took my luggage to her house the night before and her father arrived the next morning. As they were loading the luggage she told her Dad that they would have to wait an extra hour until I got out of my class because I had an important final. That day he was not a patient man and refused to wait. As I was leaving for class to take my final I received a call from my friend. She would not be able to give me a ride home.

It felt as though my heart was ripped out of my chest. I panicked. I called the bus station only to find all buses full. Tickets for buses out of the area had been sold out days previously. There were few people left on campus and it seemed that I had no way to get home but to hitchhike.

Hitchhiking was done back then but was not a popular mode of transportation. I didn't dare ask people for a ride, let alone solicit it with my thumb out.

I called my mother and, of course, she was hysterical. She inquired, "How are you getting home?" I said, "Well, the only alternative I really have is to bum a ride or hitchhike." She told me to just stay for the weekend and not come home, but being a vacation weekend, the residence hall was closed, so I couldn't stay there. I had no money for a motel so I began to hitchhike.

One of my fellow students gave me a ride into Rochester. I asked if it were south as I knew that was the direction I had to go. He said, "Well, yeah, it is." He let me out at an exit in the inner city.

There I stood at the exit on a cold November day. It was half raining and half snowing. I stuck out my thumb as I held up a sign for the city nearest my hometown. It was a busy ramp to a thoroughfare and it was difficult to get people to read the sign. No one stopped. I turned to my faith and explained the situation to God. I told Him I needed to know that I wasn't alone and that I needed help out of this nightmare.

At that moment the clouds parted and a burst of sun shone through. A beautiful rainbow appeared over the thoroughfare I was to travel. I stood gazing at the rainbow, somewhat awestruck, and suddenly a horn blasted. A man in a big white Cadillac rolled down the window and said, "Do you need a ride or don't you?" I said, "Yes, are you going south?" He said, "Yeah, I am." So I got in the car with the gentleman. I told him I was taking any sign that indicated south, hoping it would bring me near my hometown. He was from a town an hour beyond where I lived so he would be traveling through my hometown.

Whether it be answered prayers, the presence of God, fate itself, or just honest-to-goodness Irish luck, I was able to get home.

Throughout my life God has appeared at different times, sending a message to let me know that He's there and that I'm okay.

CHAPTER FIVE

The summer of 1964 found me busy touring the countryside on my bicycle looking for U.F.O.s. A man in a community fifteen miles away from us had seen a U.F.O the year before and I was dedicated to finding one. The farmer had been preparing fields when he claimed a U.F.O. landed. The spacecraft opened and a man, approximately four feet tall, got out, took samples of rock, soil, and fertilizer, got back in the spacecraft, and took off.

In his excitement, or perhaps disbelief, the farmer made the event public knowledge.

Of course, there was great publicity. Everyone chose sides whether to believe or not to believe. My immediate thought was, "Why not?" I have always believed that in His infinite wisdom God created us. He realized the frailty of human nature and that human emotion would seek to destroy humankind. Fears, jealousies, envies, and all of the deadly sins could ultimately lead to the demise of the human race. With that understanding in my heart, I began to realize that God probably placed the human animal in other parts of His galaxy as a safety precaution so that the species would endure. The people may be different in size or physical appearance because of environmental influences, but otherwise may be very much like us. Perhaps they have not busied themselves destroying one another but are advancing their own species. Therefore, they have reached us before we have reached them.

As I rode my bike looking for evidence of extraterrestrial visits, I was convinced even more of the validity of the sighting in the nearby town.

Many disbelievers couldn't understand why an alien would be interested in samples taken from the field. They laughed at the notion.

Approximately three years after the sighting, as I understand it, the witness to this event had a breakdown. This allowed greater proof that what he saw was real. We have all been in situations where we knew something to be true and others would not believe us. The feeling of betrayal, desperation, frustration, and anxiety begins to dominate. Perhaps this individual, in his desperation for someone else to believe in him, was led to an emotional breakdown.

Nevertheless, I rode the countryside looking for a space ship. Why? I'm not sure. Maybe it could take me out of the life I was in or take me to some wonderful new horizon. Perhaps I could verify this man's experience and bring him some comfort in his sighting. Through the many miles I rode I found no trace of extraterrestrials but it did not change my belief.

In July of 1969, about six years after the sighting, I watched as man landed the first spacecraft on the moon. I was excited as the astronaut emerged from the spacecraft and placed the American flag in the moon's crust. The feeling of patriotism, the goosebumps you get when the national anthem is played, added to the exhilaration of the event. It was even more exciting for me as

I watched him gather samples of rock and particles from the moon's surface, got back in the spacecraft, and took off. The focus of disbelief, six years prior, from another entity coming to earth and doing the same thing was validated by our man on the moon. We had traveled those millions of miles to take rock samples, but wouldn't believe someone else could. There is no difference between human beings and any other entity in God's creation. Our arrogance and superficiality makes us forget that God created the universe, not just planet Earth.

Years later I was doing radio shows and often would have guests appear on the show who had expertise in certain areas of psychic phenomena or mental awareness. A man who had written a book on U.F.O.s was on the show and we discussed the sightings that had taken place when I was a young man. He told me that around the same time, a similar experience had happened in Sonora, Mexico. A man was working in his fields and a spacecraft came and took rock samples. It was identical to the incident near my hometown. Although I have searched the skies and the fields in vain, seeking something or someone from beyond this world, it has not proved fruitful. However, my belief has never wavered. The only difference between myself and the young boy riding his bicycle in the movie "E.T." was that he found his extraterrestrial, I have not.

CHAPTER SIX

My mother's death was devastating to me. It came at the wrong time in my life although I suppose the death of one's mother never can come at the right time. I was beginning my senior year of college and looking forward to the freedom that my graduation would offer. Dad's alcoholism had advanced and Ma's health was rapidly failing. I hoped she would live until I graduated so I could provide for her the things she lacked her entire life. I could take care of her and bring her comfort from the suffering that had become her life.

I received the phone call that she had been taken to the hospital only three days after I had visited her at my aunt's home. Seeing Ma's health was declining quickly, my aunt decided to take care of her in her home. Ma would receive better care than she would at home with Dad.

The previous weekend I had been visiting some friends at a college upstate. On Sunday I had a feeling that I should go home to see Ma. There was an urgency to the feeling. I decided I would take Monday off, visit with her, then go back to college Monday night.

Upon arriving at my aunt's house my mother seemed okay. She had some difficulty breathing but was up and about. Her feet and legs were swollen, making it difficult for her to get around. However, she didn't seem incapacitated.

The next morning, as my aunt and uncle were busy doing their morning chores, my mother and I had a chance to be alone. She confided in me that she was dying. She knew her death was imminent. She slipped her high school ring on my little finger, saying, "Wear it as a reminder of how important education is in one's life."

She knew I was contemplating quitting school. She wanted me to finish so I wouldn't create more tragedy in the family. She said, "Every time you think of quitting school I want you to rub that ring and remember . . ."

She had graduated from the eighth grade at the one-room schoolhouse near her home and received a scholarship to go to a nearby city to high school. The scholarship paid for four years of high school education which was like a college degree. She was so proud of her diploma.

Two days after my visit I got the call to come home as Ma was in the hospital dying. My roommate offered to drive me home but his car wasn't dependable. I chose to ride the bus so I could be alone with my thoughts.

It was a long ride home with lots of time to think. I thought of all the good times, all the difficult times, and how my rebellious nature had probably cast some worries on Ma that I couldn't take back.

I went directly to the hospital from the bus station. I walked into her room where Ma was sitting up in bed eating ice cream. My sister, Rose, said, "The doctor said she could have anything she wanted to eat. It's important for her to eat."

The look in Ma's eyes, as well as my sister's behavior, told me that she could have anything she wanted to eat because she was dying. I kissed her and held her hand. I asked, "How ya doin'?"

In matter-of-fact terms, with no ifs, ands, or buts about it, she looked me in the eye and said, "I'm dying."

Our eyes met and I knew. I didn't have to answer her. She knew that I knew. My eyes filled with tears and I couldn't hold my emotions much longer. I stepped into the hallway and went on to the sunroom. I sobbed my heart out. For days I couldn't bear to be in the room only a couple minutes every hour. I couldn't stand seeing my mother in this condition. Although she had been sick for the past several years, this was so very real, and I knew the end was near.

The next morning she was on oxygen. I sat in the hallway by her door and waited. Two days passed and my brother came home from college. She appeared a bit better, but it was a short time after his visit that she went into a coma and died the next morning at eight o'clock. I was at my aunt's house and had planned to be back at the hospital at eight o'clock.

My aunt had let me sleep an extra hour. I was awakened by the phone ringing. I knew, before my aunt answered it, that my mother was dead. I ran down the stairs. My aunt was looking up at me shaking her head. I thought to myself, it was the way it should have been. A mother with her two daughters at a time when the personal dignity of women should be honored. I was glad I wasn't there.

My life had changed permanently, and from that morning my life was different. I had to take what I had learned and be independent. I needed to survive.

It was like waging a battle without a general. The person who had all the answers was gone. My anger lasted for many years. I never did know who I was angry at—God, myself, or my mother. Who the hell was I angry at? I just knew I was angry. She was dead and my father, who had made her life miserable, was still living. I couldn't find justice in *that* courtroom.

On the afternoon of my mother's death I went to church. I stood before the altar, waving my fists at God in total desperation and anger. I spoke my piece, not knowing that a woman from the Altar Guild was waiting in the back of the church. She had come to prepare the altar for communion. Embarrassed, I left the church, desperate for answers. I went to visit a woman who was like a second mother to me. She did her best to console me.

I wandered aimlessly. It's a feeling you get when someone dies, like you need to do something but you don't know what. You busy yourself with most anything and you need to be around people because one of the most important people in your life has just left you.

Consolation came through a very few words that a friend said to me when I met her at another friend's small apparel shop. I often would visit there for a cup of tea in the afternoon. As I walked in I was greeted by my friend, Kay. She saw me coming down the aisle toward the back of the store. I entered the make-shift storage room/lounge. We met with a fond embrace. She hugged me and whispered in my ear, "I am so sorry Phil, but at least she's where he can't get at her."

Suddenly, there was one of those wonderful moments of truth that seldom come along but leaves such an impact. She was right. Never again would I have to hear my mother abused. Never again would I have to see her worry about life. Never again would I have to see her suffer in any way. Her suffering had ended and although she was away from us all, she certainly was where Dad could not get at her.

I mourned her death for several years. Months longer than the normal grief process should have taken.

Then one night in my apartment I awakened, sitting on the

edge of my bed with tears staining my cheeks. I had a dream, or what seemed like a dream. My mother sat beside me with her arm around my shoulders. She said to me, "You must let go of your grief for me. I've had my life and now you must have yours. Let go of it and be as happy as you can be."

My grief subsided for my mother from that moment. I was able to put her death in its proper perspective in my life.

CHAPTER SEVEN

The semester after my mother died was my final one. All that remained was my student-teaching practicum and graduation. At last, I could prove I had some smarts or at least I thought I could.

Dad's drinking worsened after Ma died. He had no one to argue with and no one to take care of him. The only thing that occupied his time was drinking. He rapidly began a descent into the final stages of alcoholism. His memory was affected and his physical health began to falter. The towering, good-looking man that I had admired in so many ways had begun to show signs that alcohol was winning the battle.

I visited home several times during the fall after Ma died. I could see Dad was getting to the point where he could not live alone. My sister, Rose, faithfully made sure he went to work as a custodian at the nearby university. She was in an early marriage and pregnant. She had all she could do to keep him going until he was able to retire. Somehow, by the grace of God, she did it.

I asked my college advisor if it would be possible to student-teach near my hometown. I explained that my mother had died and my father was ill. My two sisters were married and away, and my brother was at college. If I could live at home I could take care of my father and complete my college education. Otherwise, I was uncertain I could.

The advisor pulled some strings and I was able to do my student teaching in the nearby community of Spencer, New York. I was under the supervision of a wonderful master teacher who had taught French and was attempting to teach Spanish, the subject that I taught. I had a pleasant student-teaching experience but not such a pleasant home life. Each time I went home Dad acted as if I was visiting him for the first time. He seldom knew me but almost always thought I was his brother, Howard, who had been killed in the war. On occasions he would think I was one of his drinking buddies. He began to hallucinate different things and imagine things that were just not reality.

During my student-teaching experience many of the faculty and students discovered my interest in psychic phenomenon and approached me frequently with questions they had. I responded to the best of my knowledge in as professional a way possible as a "would-be" teacher. I completed my student teaching with satisfactory grades and graduated in May of 1972, on Mother's Day.

It was then my father's behavior became so violent that I could no longer live at home. I decided that I should look for an apartment. I would be doing permanent substitute teaching in Spencer so I looked for an apartment in town.

My decision to move was hastened one night by my father. He was drunk again and asked me if I would get out of bed and prepare him some breakfast. I remembered the countless years that he would come home drunk, at one, two, or three o'clock in the morning, awaken Ma and insist she make breakfast for him. He then abused her all the while she was cooking. He would tell her what a whore she was, what a no-good tramp, and what a poor excuse for a human being she was.

The night he asked me to get breakfast, I, of course, did not want to begin training for the role my mother had previously held. An argument ensued and he threatened to kill me. "I know I would do the world a favor if I did away with you. The world considers Philip such trash I'd get out of it with just a slap on the hand," he rambled on.

He had it all figured out and, in his drunken stupor, talked of how he would do it. "I will wait until you are asleep, then I'll take a butcher knife and stab you to death."

Although he was drunk, it sounded quite believable to me so I prepared myself that if I was going to die, he was going to prison.

I put a tape recorder under my bed, recording as I went to sleep. A few moments later, I awakened with Dad at the side of my bed holding a butcher knife over me, telling me in his loud inebriated voice that the end was here. I kicked him in the chest and knocked him from the bedroom into the kitchen, ass-over-tea cup. He dropped the knife, rose to his feet, and ran to the living room, fearful that I was going to use the weapon he had intended for me.

That was the last night I ever slept in the house that had been my home for my first twenty-two years of my life. I moved into an apartment in Spencer the next day.

I cried for days, weeks, months, and years that Dad and I could not have a relationship. It was ironic that the one despised and hated the most was the one who came home to take care of him. There must be a spiritual lesson in all this but I haven't fully come to understand it. I did the best I knew how, that was all I could do, but it was never enough.

CHAPTER EIGHT

Spencer, N.Y., is a small community with many likable people and I had gathered many friends from student-teaching. My apartment was a tiny two-room apartment. It was good to be on my own. I could make my own decisions, live my own life, and begin that journey toward happiness.

In March 1973, following student-teaching, I was asked by one of the teachers if I would speak to a class of eighteen seniors about mental telepathy. The class was called Communications and the teacher perceived telepathy as the ultimate communication. The communication of one mind to another simply through the thought process borders on science fiction. However, mental telepathy is common to most people. A person might perceive that someone is thinking about them before they call, or one will know what someone is thinking or about to say before they do so, or vice versa.

My yearning to teach was strong and I knew it would be a fun thing to do. I cautioned the teacher about public concerns about a lecture on psychic phenomenon in the school system. She had already taken care of it. The school had signed permission slips from the parents of each student. If a student did not want to sit in class they were not obligated to do so.

My lecture had such positive rapport that the teacher asked me to do a five-day workshop on developing the unconscious part of our mind, understanding telepathy, and perceiving the world in a psychic way.

Psychic is a word that means mental. Humans have placed supernatural connotations to it through some of the experiences and themes that are associated with it, but "psychic" merely means mental. It is the use of the human mental processes in a way that may be beyond the normal scope of reality and senses.

On the Thursday prior to the workshop, I received a call from the principal. He was concerned about my involvement with the Communications class. I had become acquainted with him from my student-teaching days. I assured him that I would maintain a professional attitude and do nothing to jeopardize the class or the school in the eyes of the community. He was satisfied and trusted my integrity.

The following morning I received another call from the same man. He was more concerned. He asked if I would come in to speak to him, faculty members, and two individuals concerned about my spiritual nature. I knew immediately what I was up against.

Fundamentalists, or so-called religious people, who thought that my work and my interests were of the devil had rallied.

I told him I would be there within an hour.

As I walked into the school, one of my former students was waiting for his bus to vocational school. He said to me, "You really got yourself in trouble this time, huh, Mr. Jordan?"

I looked at him, puzzled, and he said, "The auditorium is filling up with angry parents and people carrying Bibles. It looks like it's going to be quite a fight."

I proceeded through the doors and went directly to the principal's office. There I was met by the principal and the guidance counselor. They asked me if I would sit on stage in the auditorium and answer a few questions from concerned parents. I had no objections as I was sure of myself and sure of my work. I pondered the thought of me against the sixty-two people gathered in the assembly hall. I was a little outnumbered. I asked if I could call my priest to be at my side and a friend of mine came from the community. She was a member of our parish so she sat with the priest when he arrived. I went up on stage.

Two ministers sat with their Bibles on their lap. Each time they spoke they waved the Bible at the audience to emphasize the good book as if they were Billy Graham wannabe's. I listened as ignorance poured out of supposedly educated people. They were people who find it difficult to believe in anything beyond themselves. People filled with fear. A fear that drives them to want the world to be like them. I witnessed unchristian acts of supposed brotherly love, phony loving thy neighbor as thyself, and harsh judgment. I watched as they attempted to destroy me in front of the school and the community.

The meeting lasted for approximately an hour and forty-five minutes. The school administration decided that I would be allowed to come into the classroom for one class. I had to stand before the students and state that I was a practicing Christian. My discussion would be limited to the concept of mental telepathy. I thanked them for allowing me back in the classroom as I certainly wasn't going to refuse because that was exactly what they wanted. I informed the assembled people that the world outside this small, narrow-minded community was very interested in mental phenomenon. I told them, "Newspapers and the media at large will make me a well-known person. It will do exactly what you don't want it to do."

The next day the local newspaper carried an article on the

"witch hunts" in Spencer, New York. The next seven days the paper carried the story of my return to the classroom. It proved to be the publicity that gave me my start. Soon people were calling and asking me for consultations and my opinion on different matters. It was interesting that, through prayer and meditation, they weren't taught to love their enemy but rather to promote him.

The weeks ahead were difficult. One night my house was stoned and the following Halloween they killed my little Scottie terrier. At eight o'clock that evening I had received a call from a woman who was laughing. She said, "We got your dog and you will be next."

Toto had gone out before we went to bed that evening and never returned home. The neighbor boy found her the next day under a pile of rocks near the bridge.

The witch hunt continued for months. People said and did strange and bizarre things. There was no doubt if people were for or against me. They made it very obvious.

One day I was buying groceries and I walked by two women. One of them was the mother of one of my students from Spanish class the year before. As I walked by, one woman said, "There he is. There's that man. That's the man who can draw your child's brain right out of her ears."

I couldn't resist the temptation. I made a quick U-turn with my shopping cart, stopped at the ladies, and said, "Excuse me, I overheard your conversation. I presume it was intended for me. You have nothing to worry about. Your daughter was one of my students. I'm fairly certain there are no brains in her head to draw out of her ears."

I turned and finished my shopping.

Ironically, the witch hunt and heresy trials were an incidental event to what would transpire in the town of Spencer, New York regarding my career. The publicity concerning the incident, coupled with severe unemployment, helped me to decide to offer psychic consultations to the general public. Money was scarce but I was able to muster up a few bucks and put a two-dollar ad in the local Shopper. Soon I was receiving calls and people were stopping by for personal consultation. After a few weeks I decided to go into business, but only until I was able to secure a teaching position. I became so busy that I rented an office in my hometown. In weeks I had a regularly scheduled clientele and was receiving inquiries from newspapers, radio, and television stations.

One of the local newspapers asked if I would be open to a test of my psychic abilities. I agreed. I went to the small community that they designated for the experiment.

They had taken a staple-puller off the mayor's desk. They showed it to me and let me touch it. A police officer took me out of town while they hid the staple-puller. Within minutes after returning I was able to locate it. It was hidden in the top of a propane gas tank, behind a building, a block from the mayor's office. It was a great human interest story. Things seemed to be going very good.

On August 4, 1975, my life changed again. I had traveled to a house party fifty miles away across the border into Pennsylvania. I returned home in the early evening hours during a severe thunderstorm. The fire whistle began to blare as I parked the car in the garage, calling all volunteer firemen to the station. I assumed, with the severity of the storm, that lightning had struck somewhere and ignited a fire.

I ran across the backyard in the downpour. As I passed the back porch the landlady yelled to me. "What's all the commotion?" I asked, knowing that her husband was a fire policeman.

She said, "A six-year-old boy is missing at Empire Lake. He was last seen wearing a swimsuit and carrying an inflatable swim toy. He wandered away from his family and they fear he went into the lake and drowned."

Empire Lake is a huge man-made lake and recreational facility for the state university. During the summer months, people who visit the lake enjoy nude swimming. It had become quite a place of conversation for the local people.

Suddenly, a vision came to me. "I can see the boy. He's sleeping with his head on his right arm under a tree. He's alive. He's not in the water. If he's in the water it would have to be under a tree under the water. The tree is a living tree in the outdoors so I don't think he has drowned. When your husband comes home let me know the status of the case."

Shortly after going to my apartment I received a phone call about the missing boy. He was still missing. Did I have any further impressions?

It's difficult to keep your emotional involvement from overtaking your psychic investigative skills, especially when a child is missing. The eagerness to find the child immediately and remove him from all danger involves so much intensity that all thoughts stay in the conscious mind and cannot go into the unconscious mind.

I stay in a meditative unconscious mind by silent prayer. That night I was praying and I knew the child was still alive. I had been directed to a Bible verse which reaffirmed my feelings. The verse mentioned the woods.

Shortly after prayerful reassurance, I received a phone call from the boy's father. Tommy's father, Don Kennedy, had read about me in the local newspaper. He had read the story in which I had found the staple-puller. He thought that if I could find a staple-puller in an entire community, I should be able to find his son in the dense woods of upstate New York.

He asked if I would come immediately to the scene and attempt to locate his missing son. The thunderstorms continued in the area. Hope turned to fear. It was now 1:00 a.m. I had to follow the path of better judgment rather than the immediate need to help. I hesitantly told Tommy's father, "I will come as soon as it is daylight. I am fearful that I will miss a clue in my search during the night hours."

The next morning, at 5:00 a.m., my landlord, Richard, and I went to the scene. We learned there had been two hundred rescue personnel searching through the night, but to no avail.

At the scene I was greeted by the Senior Investigator from the County Sheriff's Department, a lifetime friend, David Redsicker. As we talked, I scanned the area and tried to decide in which direction Tommy might be located. Several people assisting in the search tried to sway me to a lake search. They were certain he was in the lake. I never entertained the idea that he had drowned.

I referred to a map that I had drawn in the night. A crude map, but yet a map that I used on that August 5th morning in 1975.

On the map I had drawn a lake in the shape of the lake that was actually there, although I had never been there. I had drawn three overturned boats and across the lake from them I had drawn a wooded area surrounding a small dwelling.

At the scene that morning I glanced to my left. Along the shore of the lake there were three overturned rowboats that had been used during the night in the search for Tommy's body. I looked across the lake. In the morning mist I saw a large wall tent which had obviously been placed there by people camping for their own recreation. It was completely surrounded by woods. I knew I would have to go behind the tent to locate young Tommy. I told David that I would begin my search there.

As we walked away from earshot of everybody else, David said I was going in the opposite direction from which Tommy was last seen. No one had searched that area and, being on the other side of the lake, my chances for success might be hampered. David was being kind to me, not wanting me to embarrass myself in front of all the searchers. I assured him that was where I had to go. He knew me well and knew that's where I had to go.

We started across an earthen dike to go around the lake when two young men ran up to us. They asked if they could accompany us on the search. I said okay, although I'm uncertain why they wanted to go. I think it intrigued them as to how psychics work and what we might do in the thick woods.

The search began directly behind the large wall tent. We climbed a trail and were a few minutes into the search when we looked at the map. I told the group, "We have to find a clearing with a large rock. We'll proceed beyond that clearing and find a stream that will go into waterfalls. Beyond the waterfalls there will be a field. In the edge of that field there should be a tree with Tommy Kennedy under it."

At this point I became aware of time. On the way to the scene that morning I told Richard we would find him in less than an hour. We proceeded along the trail, the two young men trying desperately to convince me that everything I was seeing was in another spot seven miles to the southwest. They tried to get me to go there. We could return to this spot in the afternoon. I didn't want to walk all day around the woods. I wanted to secure Tommy Kennedy as quickly as possible.

They almost had me convinced that I should go to the other site because of the landmarks that I had designated. Just as I was ready to give up, I looked down and saw the footprint of a young barefoot human headed up the trail. I called to the others and they verified what I was seeing.

We continued until we found a clearing. There was one large rock in the clearing but around that rock were piled other rocks, as if someone was getting ready to make a stone-based lean-to. This was the clearing that I had seen the preceding night. We moved down a path that led from the clearing until we could hear the sound of water in the woods ahead. We found a ravine and within minutes found the waterfalls that I had envisioned. I went to the bottom of the ravine in case Tommy had fallen and was seriously injured. I had been on the local ambulance squad for a few years and was the only one in the group that had first-aid training. I told Dick and the others to keep yelling. "Yell both his first and last name. If he's in shock he might recognize one or the other or both together," I encouraged.

I could not hear any noises from outside the area of the ravine.

Soon the young man who had tried to convince me to go to the other location yelled. I could tell by his voice that he believed he had heard something. He screamed, "He's yelling for help. I hear him yelling. He's yelling for help."

I immediately hollered to my friend, "Dick, do you hear him?" Dick's response was no.

I said, "Yell his name, both first and last."

Dick yelled three more times and the third time he responded in an excited voice, "I hear him yelling, he's yelling for help."

They ran toward the sound of Tommy's voice. I was climbing out of the ravine. I didn't want to lose sight of the rescuers. They ran down a slope, through the wooded area. A brightly sunlit spot could be seen through the trees. I ran down the same slope about thirty seconds behind them. They climbed over a fence and I, in my haste, vaulted the fence. There, in the clearing of a field, under a tree, were the rescuers with Tommy Kennedy.

During the somewhat less than Olympic-style fence vaulting I had sprained my lower back and left leg. Tommy was in much better shape. There he stood, clad only in his swimsuit, clutching the inflatable swim toy. There I stood holding a picture of Tommy Kennedy and a sneaker that his mother had given me.

I knelt and crossed myself, thanking God that he had given me a gift that I had used to save Tommy's life. I wept openly. All the emotions that were stirred within came to the surface. We walked through the chatter of walkie-talkies to the rescue ambulance. I will never forget the sense of pride, the feeling of accomplishment, and the air of self-worth that I had that day. It was then that I proved my abilities to myself and never again would I doubt the gifts and the talents that I had been given.

We continued our short trek to the waiting ambulance, passing an old open well. Tommy had obviously passed it in the dark. He could have fallen to his death. The sense of dread that the imposing forest gave to an adult, let alone a six-year-old child, made me very thankful that we were able to locate Tommy before any more time had elapsed.

It was actually four days after finding Tommy before my feet came back to Earth. The cheers of acknowledgment, the pats on the back, and the comfort given to me by family and friends for a job well done certainly seemed to be a long-awaited embrace.

As I reflect on the days of the search I remember the thoughts of many people.

I went to the local American Legion with some friends the night after the search had so happily ended. A man there insisted that I had hypnotized Tommy Kennedy and tied him to a tree and then went in and found him. It was unbelievable that he would think, after knowing me all my life, that I would stoop to such depths to get people to believe in me. I called on the memory of seeing Tommy under that tree. Once again I was assured that it didn't matter what others thought.

Ray Ayers, the Tioga County Sheriff, sent word through his investigators that he wanted to see me, to thank me for a job well done. I arranged a meeting with him and nervously went to his office. He made me feel comfortable and welcome.

Being the child of an alcoholic I fear authority figures. Our sheriff, a retired state trooper, was the tallest man I had ever seen in my life. It made me a bit nervous. I sat across the desk from him and he said, "What you did was a wonderful thing. I don't believe in any of that stuff but I know what I saw. I was wondering if you would allow me to have you be deputized to work with our boys in any similar cases, or *any* cases, for that matter. I know you could be of help."

I couldn't believe what I was hearing.

Six years earlier I had gone for a reading with a medium. She told me she saw me in uniform in front of the flag taking an oath. My immediate fear was that I would serve in Vietnam, but instead, 6 years later, I graduated from Municipal Police Academy, standing in front of the flag, taking my oath as a deputy.

Since that time I have worked cases for federal, state, and local agencies throughout the United States and Canada. I have found great satisfaction in piecing together some of the unsolved crimes and immediate-need cases that have baffled police officers throughout this part of the world. The search for Tommy Kennedy made me aware of how I work, what my mind can and cannot do. I now understand the procedures in search-and-rescue and the human need to be involved in such incidences. I have confronted skepticism and fears about psychics in police work. To the Tommy Kennedy incident of August 4th and 5th, 1975, to Tommy Kennedy, and all those involved, I shall be forever thankful.

CHAPTER NINE

The town that tried to destroy me became the proving ground for my abilities and a lifetime career in psychic phenomenon. The community was filled with fearful and skeptical people, but there were enough people filled with love. What started as a destructive inquisition three years earlier was hailed coast to coast through national network news. The story of a man saving a young boy's life in an uncanny way crossed the nation.

I have found it intriguing and amazing that humans will rely on specially trained dogs that utilize their instincts beyond their common senses to find missing or deceased people, drugs, or evidence to a case. Yet when a man, such as myself, comes into a case seeming to blend commonsense, unique ability, and extreme instinct, it cannot be considered as reality. Perhaps if I had a harness and leash and crawled on all fours with my nose to the ground my searches might be more believable. The successes in finding lost jewelry, missing weapons, lost or deceased persons, helps me accept myself for who I am, whether anyone else does or not.

Search dogs do remarkable things, greatly enhancing the

search effort. Every possible measure should be taken to assist, especially with a missing person who may be in danger.

Psychics are often called into a case as a last-ditch effort and all investigative leads are depleted. The investigation may have been active for weeks, months, or years, ignoring that the immediate involvement of a sensitive could help to secure evidence to the case. That seems to be an occupational hazard of being a psychic investigator. People that understand my abilities know that I will do the best I can no matter how long it's been or what the case involves.

I can't discredit anyone for rejecting the idea of using psychics in investigation. There is a thin line between psychic and psychotic. In most of my cases there are people that appear to be just a little bit off-center who volunteer information on cases. The information may be anything from kidnapping by a U.F.O. to disappearance into thin air. Again, commonsense must prevail.

Skepticism is a good keeper. It always helps to maintain a professional attitude in regards to psychic investigation. It is better not to use a psychic than someone that may discredit the investigation. A psychic trained to the techniques of police procedure understands those procedures. These sensitives do not want to lead the investigation, but add something to it. The psychic wanting to take over the case becomes bizarre in his or her thoughts and behaviors concerning the case and should not be involved. Skepticism should be as much a part of the investigation as fact in the matter.

Skepticism generally grows in the garden of fear. People are unable to accept things beyond their own grasp and cannot comprehend how something they do not understand can work. Skepticism and fear are healthy and protective to a point, but like many things they have their boundaries. People have gone beyond the bounds of skepticism and fear and have created a hypocrisy to the truth they seek. The overt skeptic or fearful person will go far beyond reality, beyond the feasibility of psychic awareness, to make something that seems unknown not true. The search for truth travels into the ridiculous or touches ignorance for fear that something unexplainable could be a part of the world.

Many people, especially those touched with a specific religious discipline, cannot allow themselves to go beyond what they or their spiritual leader may know. They cannot venture or risk their faith.

There are skeptics who yearn to have an awareness beyond their own reality, but they want everything proven to them and they go about it in the wrong way. Instead of objectively observing and considering the possibilities with an open mind, they take an immediate stand to prove that something cannot exist. They confuse the world of magic and creative deception with the world of mysticism, spiritual rapport, and harmony. They often denigrate themselves rather than the object of their intent.

The most obvious skepticism appears in the person who feels that psychic phenomenon betrays their religious, spiritual, or philosophical belief. They endeavor to figure out how psychics obtain the information that they expound to their listening audience.

Several years ago a fundamentalist church in our area was hosting a summer lecture by a Doctor of Divinity from New Jersey. The title of the lecture was "How Psychics Do It." I knew I was not welcome but my interest was great, so I chose to attend the lecture.

I sat in the sanctuary of the church among two hundred people. There were doctors and nurses, lawyers, common laborers, farmers, all people on the path they had chosen for their life journey.

I seated myself a third of the way down on the left-hand side of the aisle. The sanctuary filled with those intrigued in hearing

"How Psychics Do It." I took note that there was a capacity crowd except for the seats in front of me, to each side of me, and behind me. There was room for three to four people either side of me, in front of me, or in back of me. It would have been fun to have an aerial photo of the congregation that evening.

The Doctor of Divinity stood up at the appropriate time in the lecture (which was actually a church service). He began by telling us that we were "nothing but bloody abortions at the feet of God." I resented that as I held myself in much higher regard. I then remembered that this denomination has to suffer to inherit the Kingdom of Heaven. I realized from whence he came. He had to make people feel unworthy to be living, let alone near the Kingdom of God.

He then started to reveal the secrets of the psychics. Actually, this man, knowledgeable enough to receive a Doctor of Divinity, had confused magic and psychic phenomenon. He revealed several magic tricks and then talked about stage psychics. He revealed there are at least two ways psychics work. The pastor announced, "There is one of them in this community." He continued, "For $11.95, a measly twelve bucks, in any magic shop, you can buy a small electronic cube and a hearing device. The cube has dials to set a date for which you want information. The psychic points the device at anyone and it reveals information about them on the date that is in question. The information is relayed to an inner ear hearing apparatus and the psychic tells the audience what the particular person did on that specific day from their past."

I was dumbstruck. I couldn't believe that a supposedly intellectual human being could believe such a device existed, especially for $11.95. I watched as the anxious crowd regarded that knowledge as fact.

He explained how a psychic does a floor show or assembly.

He rambled on, "The psychic goes into an area disguised as another individual a week before the program. He goes door-to-door selling Bibles. As part of the sales agreement, he records the family history in the appropriate record section of the Bible. Through this he discovers information about the people. They attend a show and he remembers and regurgitates that information during the performance. Regurgitate is an appropriate word as, by the time I had heard this, that is exactly what I wanted to do.

It's interesting that people will believe something so preposterous so as not to acknowledge a talent or gift. The fear of something they don't understand, or something they believe demonic or satanic, helps me understand why they are so frightened.

I became fearful at the control this individual had over two hundred people. I thought of the tragedies that have occurred to people. People led in their spiritual journey by someone who may not be on a socially acceptable path. The tragedy at Jonestown, Waco, Texas, and the tragedy with the Haille-Bopp Comet transpired from people wanting to believe something a little more far-reaching than our natural instinct.

A couple years later I was doing a nightclub performance at a hotel in the heart of the Finger Lakes. It was a late Sunday afternoon show. The audience was wonderful. Everything was going great. I encouraged the audience to ask questions. That's how questions get answered—by posing them.

Two young men were at the bar, slightly intoxicated. They drank their beer and watched the show. They were quite intrigued. Suddenly one of them blurted out, "Tell me something about myself."

So I began to read on him. "You have a small white car that is a convertible. The door on the passenger side has a small dent in it."

I perceived the license number and revealed the three letters and three digits of the license number. At first he was astounded because I was correct. Then he became accusatory. I had correctly given his license number and described his vehicle but it seemed obvious to him that I had someone outside watching vehicles as they parked in the parking lot.

I assured him I didn't indulge in such trickery. The audience was confident in my honesty. They also knew the two men came in late and I had been performing for twenty minutes. The audience was certain I had not obtained the information illegitimately.

His friend tapped him on the shoulder and said, "Jim, you better shut up, you don't know what you're talking about."

Jim began to refute the friend but the friend interrupted, "We came here in my car, yours is home locked in the garage, and there is a dent in the passenger's door."

The crowd went wild as the skeptic hit the dance floor of embarrassment to the tune of "the bigger they are the harder they fall."

Skepticism is throughout humankind. Professional people maintain dignified and somewhat reserved attitudes when they think something cannot be true.

One such case was an arson of an attorney's home. I identified three areas of the home in which the fire was set, as well as a burglary of several items from the house. I named the items specifically. The accuracy of the report sent to the investigating agency brought me to the scene to ascertain more information.

I do not cross lines of investigation with police agencies. I attempt to secure the location of evidence or individuals involved that may resolve the case.

I went to the scene a week later. By that time, the county agency had elicited the aid of another policing department. The assisting agency was a state agency in which investigations are conducted in a strictly disciplined and professional manner. The new agency would never consider the use of a psychic or, for that matter, anyone outside their organization. However, I was already involved. I was at the scene of the crime when an official from the state agency arrived. He was a lieutenant.

Before the fire, there was a mother German Shepherd with puppies in the basement of the house. When the firefighters arrived they found the mother dog and puppies safely contained in an abandoned car across the yard.

The skeptical investigator inquired of my thoughts regarding the case.

I said, "I think the burglars had some kindness in their heart and got the dog and her puppies out before torching the house. To safeguard, they put the puppies in the car with the mother following. It was obviously somebody who had been around dogs."

Near the burned house lay a dead beagle. It's head had been bludgeoned. The dog was on a long chain attached to its dog house.

He asked my opinion concerning the beagle. "I think the beagle was a yippee dog that made lots of noise. To quiet the dog they bludgeoned it to death."

I told him the origin points of the fires. They had already been verified by the first investigator. I gave other bits of information pertinent to the case. Suddenly, the skeptical investigator looked at me and said it was the most preposterous thing he had ever heard. His skepticism turned into rage. To quell the rage I asked him to explain his thoughts concerning the dogs and the fire. He gave the following account:

The burglary took place as I had suggested. The missing items were obviously items that would be taken in any burglary. The mother dog and her pups were in the basement as the burglars set fire to the house above them. Having just had puppies, the mother had heightened instincts and was aware of immediate danger. She took the puppies in her mouth one by one, placing them in the abandoned automobile for protection. She then got in with them.

It was a bit unbelievable that a mother dog could go through a door at the top of the cellar, a door from the kitchen to the back porch, another door from the back porch to the outside, open a car door, put the dogs in, and get four or five pups out of harm's way before the fire consumed them. I decided at that point if this man truly believed that I would let him.

I inquired about the beagle's death. He confidently continued, "The beagle's instinct to survive had diminished with the fire being so close to its doghouse. The beagle decided to take its own life. He ran to the end of the fifty-foot chain and ran as fast as he could, bashing its head into the doghouse and taking its own life before it perished in the fire."

In an excited voice I said to the investigator, "And the only reason the mother dog didn't go back in and get the car keys hanging on the end of the cupboard was because the fire was so hot she couldn't. Otherwise she could have driven downtown and reported the fire!"

He knew what I was saying to him and I understood what he was telling me. Nothing more was said to one another. Once again, it affirmed that when something defies explanation the human need to explain is still there.

Skepticism is often passed off as coincidence. For me, there is no such thing as coincidence. Coincidences are footnotes along the pathway of life. They are guide posts at intricate times in our life. We should listen to coincidence. It may be part of the mysteries of life or a message from an unseen force greater than ourselves. To ignore them as mere coincidence may be to neglect our inner self, the nature of our own spirit, or an important turn in our life. Of course, we shouldn't allow coincidence and superstition to control our lives.

Superstitions may have had an original purpose that has been carried to extreme. I would not allow them to deter my life, but I do not walk under ladders—something might fall on my head.

Coincidence is an indication that our psychic self is actively working. We may continuously think of someone we haven't seen and suddenly, after years of absence from this person's life, they cross our path. It means *pay attention*. Something concerning that person's involvement in your life may arrive. It may mean that telepathically the person lets you know they were coming into your life before they did. Precognitively speaking, you may have known that person was coming into your life. Whatever, it is not coincidence. Your mind has allowed that event to occur for a reason.

The great spirit we call God is busy at work maintaining His creation at all times. Each time I perform a wedding as the pastor of our church, conduct a funeral, or baptise a child, I'm aware that the church is blessing a series of events that have led the person to that precise moment. A couple standing before God's altar, one born in Florida and one in Massachusetts, sees that only through circumstances beyond their control (or coincidence, if you will), they crossed each other's path and discovered their love for each other—God maintaining His creation rather than creating coincidence. God knew their love for each other long before they did and brought them together, and by no coincidence.

I remember talking to a couple who had been stranded in an airport together during a blizzard. They exchanged addresses and decided to write. The letters soon became love letters. The love letters soon became vows of marriage. Perhaps a coincidence that both were traveling at exactly the same time, at exactly the same airport, but it's wonderful to believe that through the assistance of Mother Nature, God brought them together.

Unfortunately, coincidence is seen concerning the death of people. People at exactly the right place, at exactly the right time (or exactly the wrong time), resulting in a tragedy that results in their death. It is difficult to comprehend unless we rest in faith that what led to the events of death were beyond coincidence. God does not inflict suffering upon His creation. Death is a fact of life.

I am often asked about suffering. Suffering is an earthly condition. It is often an affliction connected to our physical being but touches our spiritual reality and emotional self. Through suffering it may be easier for a person to let go of life and for life to let go of the person.

Of all the people I have seen suffer, it becomes not only a cry but a prayer that suffering will end for the person I have loved. The suffering person allows that pain to help them to let go of the life to which they cling. Through faith they inherit a new life, free of the bondage and suffering of the present. Just as the trees, plants, and animals have their seasons in life, so do we. In simple faith we must understand that and allow ourselves to be content through the seasons as they unfold. As we travel the highways and byways of life, we must keep an eye on the guide posts and pay attention to the road ahead. We never know when the road will take a sudden turn. It may be prompted through so-called coincidence, an act of nature, or divine intervention. Whatever, pay attention so you can fulfill your promise to creation.

CHAPTER TEN

Most every family has its own ghost stories. Tales from the past passed from generation to generation, embellished a bit for the sake of storytelling, holding truth that intrigues every ear. My family is no exception when it comes to ghost stories.

I first became aware of some of the supernatural mysteries in life during my teenage years. Our great grandmother came from Ireland. She was very gifted psychically, very aware of the world around her both seen and unseen. Since her arrival in the States in the late 1840s, during Ireland's potato famine, each generation has shared some wonderful mysteries. She didn't create these mysteries but left an open-minded spirituality that allowed each generation to believe there is more in life and beyond than we perceive.

Psychic awareness, and the need to survive, compliment each other well. Both often appear through some traumatic experience.

One hot summer day, when my mother was eleven years old, she learned all about instinct, psychic things, and survival.

A storm was brewing from the west so she decided to pump a pitcher of water before the storm. She grabbed the metal handle of the pitcher pump. Suddenly she was knocked unconscious. Lightning had struck a wire clothes line that was attached to the post on the pumping stand. It knocked her free of the pumping stand but into a deep unconsciousness.

Her sister, Florence, eighteen years older than her, heard the calamity and ran to her side. She was sure her little sister had been killed. She picked up the limp body in her arms and ran to the barn across the road. Their Mom and Dad were doing chores. Her mother grabbed the unconscious child, ran to the icehouse, removed a couple of cakes of ice, and laid her daughter's injured body in the bed of ice. Apparently, this immediately lowered her body temperature and saved her life. She regained consciousness without severe damage, but had little memory of the four hours of unconsciousness.

My grandmother's only medical training was in the homeopathy of rural America. She said she didn't know what to do, but instinctively knew what she needed to do. Thus it saved her little Myrtle's life.

Perhaps it was surviving this near-death incident that awakened my mother's acute psychic perception.

A few summers later, my mother's brother, William Henry, was in a rocking chair on a second floor porch waiting for a storm to pass. Lightning hit the base of the chair, knocking him over backwards and through a screen door. The family ran to the second floor to see what the commotion was all about. William Henry was standing dazed but unscathed. So I guess lightning does strike twice in the same place. These two hits were approximately twenty feet apart.

My maternal great-grandfather volunteered for the Civil War, at the age of fourteen. He lied about his age. Men could not engage in battle until the age of sixteen, but he was determined to prove himself a soldier in the battles between the North and the

South. His true age was never discovered but his youthful appearance apparently took him away from being a gun-toting soldier as he became a drummer for the regiment as they marched from battle to battle.

As the war progressed he developed a special comradeship with another soldier. The friendship grew into a special buddy relationship. The two became inseparable. They could rely on each other for strength and courage and became confidants, one to the other.

One day, the two friends had become separated from the other men in the regiment. They discovered that the regiment had moved further on due to an impending battle.

The two soldiers walked along a country road in search of their regiment as night descended. They decided to take rest and refuge for the night rather than to wander around unknown territory looking for their fellow soldiers. They sought cover under a large oak tree and began to bed down. As they were preparing their beds my grandfather had an uneasiness come over him. A feeling of danger was around them. He shared his feelings with his friend. The other soldier mocked him as my grandfather pleaded for them to continue their journey. The uneasiness grew more intense. Granddad made the decision to go on by himself. He said to his friend, "I cannot stay here. I'm going further down the road and I'll wait 'til you catch up in the morning."

He went down the road about a mile and a half until he felt the uneasiness subside. There, he set up a makeshift camp and stayed until the dawn beckoned the morning skies.

During the night there had been a brief thunderstorm but he arose unscathed and dry. He waited for his friend. Soon he became restless. The friend did not join him. After a couple of hours of anguished anticipation he retraced his steps. In the distance he could see the tall oak tree and his friend lying under it. He yelled to his friend—no answer. He approached the tree and his eyes met with a horrific scene. There, under the tree, as if asleep, lay his friend. He was dead. Granddad looked above the lifeless body. One side of the tree was charred and still casting small curls of smoke into the air. Lightning had struck the tree during the brief storm in the night. His friend had been electrocuted by the bolt of lightning. Granddad's premonition of danger had served him well. He, too, would have been under the tree and most certainly dead.

I have often thought of that story since it was told to me. Granddad trusted his psychic self and endured the battles of the Civil War. He certainly would not have won the battle against Mother Nature. Had he stayed under the tree that night I would not be here telling the story.

It is evident to me that psychic intuitiveness and premonition are carried from generation to generation. They are unconsciously taught as a trait of protection and spiritual growth. Each time I read the Christmas story about the birth of Christ, I am reminded of the story of Joseph. Joseph received information in a dream or from an angel of the Lord where he was told to remove the Christ Child from the jurisdiction of Herod.

The bond of love that Joseph had for his newborn son was a bond of protection, a bond that would help him to be aware of danger around his family. Whether the information came in a dream or through an angel of the Lord (which could have been a spirit entity around him) doesn't matter. He received a mental impression, a psychic impression, if you will, that saved the life of the infant Christ and thus saved Christian religion.

Many fundamentalists dispute this as a psychic occurrence, but it was a mental phenomenon in which Joseph trusted. He acted on his own feelings toward a certainty that he must act. Though fundamentalists will not agree, the Bible is full of wonderful stories of psychic events and angelic attributions that have not only enhanced the Biblical tales but served important events of Christian faith and growth.

Years ago, when I was having troubles with fundamentalists regarding my teaching and beliefs, the oldest woman in our church invited me to her home for tea. I was fearful that she would say something to me that would mar my impression of her. She was one of the sweetest old ladies that I had ever known.

She had the table delightfully set with two of her best china cups. A small platter of homemade sugar cookies with raisins thumbed in the centers sat between the two cups. She poured the tea from a flowered china teapot.

She said, "I am aware of the problems you are having with people concerning your gifts. I want you to be strong and carry those gifts as God has asked you to do. Never let anyone take a gift from you that God has given you. He intended for you to have the gift. He has chosen you to carry it because he knows that you are able to do so."

She dabbed her lips with her napkin and continued, "The people that are against you are filled with fear, that's their problem. They think people with prophetic abilities are only in the Old Testament or when Christ walked among us. Christ was an example for us of God in human form, an example of a person who shared His gifts. If they think those people can only exist in old times, they're mistaken. They had better get with the times and realize that there are many wonderfully talented and gifted people in the world today. My love and support is with you."

My eyes filled with tears as her love spoke in such frank and easy terms. It was a note of approval that I needed at that moment. It was a hand of love reaching out to me that I shall never forget. It has been several years since she died, but the warmth of those tender moments has never left me.

Having a bit of Irish blood in our veins has not hindered psychic development. Our Irish grandmother came to the United States and settled in the northeastern part of Pennsylvania, close to the New York border, not awfully far from where I now live.

In late April of 1966, I was awakened one spring morning by the sounds of the birds chirping outside my window. It was time to get up. Beams of sunlight were casting a cascade of light upon my dresser. I followed them from the window to the dresser. As I moved in the bed particles of dust danced as if they were tiny diamonds reflecting the warmth of the early morning sun.

I looked at my dresser and there sat a small man. He had red hair and beard, he was dressed in a suit, and had on very strange shoes.

I rubbed my eyes, thinking that it was my imagination. Perhaps I was dreaming that there was a little man sitting on my dresser which was in disarray. The drawers were pulled out in almost perfect step fashion.

I rubbed my eyes a second time. The man was still there. He was about eighteen or twenty inches tall and had all the features of a normal man. I watched as he climbed down, using the dresser drawers. He stood in an area between my bed and my father's bed. He put his hands on his hips, looked up at me, and in a squeaky voice said, "My name is Joz and I will see you one more time before you die."

My heart was throbbing in my throat. I wondered if it meant I was going to die or if he was going to be with me for a long life. He skipped off and ran down the stairs. I chased after him. I ran down the stairs, through the bathroom, and into the dining room. Ma was cooking at the kitchen stove. She turned around and saw the perplexity on my face. She asked, "What's wrong?"

I explained to her what had happened. She said, "You have

seen one of the little people or the wee people as they are called in Ireland. They will be with you throughout your life, but you may not always be able to see them."

She told me the story about her great-grandmother. Grandma McDuffy had brought seven leprechauns with her from Ireland in the hem of her skirt. The day she died, one of the last things she said was that all seven leprechauns were on the pillow around her head. She then went through the gate of death.

Ma continued, "You will realize a very special gift in the near future."

Six weeks later I had the dream about my uncle having a heart attack. The dream sent me on my adventure into the world of the unknown.

I do not tell that story often for fear people would think I'd lost my mind. However, I did share it on a radio show one St. Patrick's Day. Five people called to tell me of similar experiences.

One man, who appeared to be a very sane, adult professional, called to tell me of his experience while fishing in the Adirondack Mountains in upstate New York. After fishing all day, this man sat down for a short rest. He looked to his right and there, sitting on the bank beside him, was a wee person. He was similar in appearance to what I just described. The little man looked up at the fisherman and said, "You don't believe I'm here, do you?"

The man shook his head and rubbed his eyes in disbelief. The little man got up, walked out across the water a short distance, walked back and sat down. He said, "Don't worry, I'm with you for a long time," and then disappeared.

Whether the wee people are spiritual manifestations or actual beings doesn't matter to me. It's a spiritual joy for me to have the understanding and belief that the love God sends me comes in different packages and it's not just in this physical world but in the spiritual world. It's comforting.

There is another Irish tradition called the Banshee. The Banshee is similar to the mythological characters the Sirens. The Banshee is the spirit of a woman that beckons people to inform them of a death. She is always heard to lament at a distance. It is a lamentation that draws you near to it as if to take note that something in your life is about to change. It warns that someone around you may be about to die and will have a direct effect on your life. If you hear a Banshee, take heed. Prepare yourself! If you ever see a Banshee never look her in the eyes for it will be certain that you will be the one to die.

On three different occasions I have heard Banshees. Two times were prior to the death of a cousin and an uncle. One time was at the death of an aunt.

I was warned of my aunt's death one afternoon while having tea at a friend's home. Suddenly, I could hear the call of the Banshee. I must have had a peculiar look on my face as the hostess asked me what was wrong. "You look like you have just seen a ghost."

I responded, "I don't think I have seen one but I am sure that I had heard one."

I explained the story of the Banshee, assuring her that within three days I would hear of a death. Twenty-four hours later my aunt died.

I share these stories for several reasons. I find them interesting to my own soul and I want to share them as part of our family heritage as I believe there are many things in life we can't explain. Whether it be a manifestation of my own mind, my psychic self alerting me to an impending death, or whether it be a spirit foretelling of life's experience, doesn't matter to me. Whether people believe me or not can't negate the experience. I have discovered some seemingly unreal things in this real world.

When I was a young lad of seven, I was having toast one

morning with my mother when she said to me, "One of the neighbors died last night."

I wondered how she knew that. We had been sleeping all night and we had no telephone. I knew no one had been to the house for I had awakened at the same time as my mother. I asked her how she knew that. She said, "I had a dream in the night that the death coach came down the street, turned around at the end of the street, and came back out. It stopped in the middle of our street. The driver got off the seat, opened the carriage door, left it open for a few moments, and then closed it."

I was finishing my toast and hot chocolate when a neighbor knocked at the door. Ma opened the door. The neighbor talked through the screen door. She said, "I just wanted to stop by and tell you that Tink (the old man down the street) died in the night. We're taking up a collection from the neighborhood for flowers."

I was mystified. Ma was right. How did she know these things?

I think her life of misery and suffering facilitated an unconscious way to know and understand the world around her. Ma was an intelligent woman but it seemed that her intelligence went beyond its own nature. She had a gifted insight that defied human explanation. She talked about her dreams in a way that showed me how important it was that we be aware of our mind, not only as we're awake, but as we sleep. We should understand that our mind will continue to work for us in sleep by allowing us knowledge that we may not be aware of when awake.

A few years later I had another unusual experience.

When one of the family became ill and needed a doctor (and trust me we had to be in need of a doctor because of our financial situation), we would travel to a country doctor fifteen miles away. Some of his ideas were a bit peculiar but yet he was a good doctor.

He was a grandfatherly type who never took the world too seriously but always seemed to know how to make you feel better. His procedures were a bit antiquated, but yet he seemed to always get us back on the road to recovery.

Once, while we were waiting in his office, a man was resting on the daybed in the bay window at the end of the waiting room. I noticed he had an odd color. Part of his face seemed ashen gray and white, part of his face seemed to be purple and blue. My aunt and mother were talking in signals to each other, hoping I wouldn't notice. Their secrecy was divulged when the doctor beckoned us to the office. He began to ask what was wrong with me. My mother, nervously, interrupted. She said, "There's a man lying on the daybed in the waiting room. It appears he's not well at all."

Without hesitation the good doctor said, "Oh, him, he died about an hour ago and we're just waiting for the coroner and the funeral director to come and remove the body."

I remember the look of horror on my mother's face as she suggested that they might want to throw a sheet over him as a gesture of comfort to the others in the waiting room.

Another visit to the good doctor was to treat my infected ingrown toenails, one on each big toe. They had become so infected and sore that I was becoming limited in my ability to walk. My aunt decided I must see the doctor. He put me in a reclined chair, bringing my feet to where he could look at them. He touched them. The soreness was so intense that I yelped. He rubbed his chin and said he was pretty sure he could take care of them. He went to a small room off the examining room and came back with a pair of snubbed-nose electrician's pliers.

He latched on to the toenail on my right foot and ran the blunt-nosed pliers under the nail and ripped it off. The pain traveled like a jolt of electricity from my toe all the way to my head. I immediately fainted.

I mysteriously found myself walking into a barn where a beautiful woman was milking a cow. The woman had dark brown hair piled on her head in a bun, a Gibson Girl appearance. She wore a long skirt with a wide-banded waist and a blouse. She got up from her milking and embraced me. She said, "Philip, what are you doing here? You're not supposed to be here. You've got to be out of here. We love you but go back and do the things you have to do."

I couldn't understand what she meant by going back and doing the things I had to do. Suddenly I was back in the doctor's chair experiencing the pain of the moment.

Several months, if not years, later I found a picture of that woman. The moment I saw the picture I knew it was her. I asked Ma who it was and discovered it to be a picture of her mother in her younger days. Apparently, I had been with her prematurely and was unable to stay.

I didn't know my grandmother, as she died four years before I was born. I do know the warmth and love that she must have given her family for many years and I now know her as if I had grown with her in my life all the time.

The pain in my toe subsided immediately and the doctor began to work on the other foot. My anxious mother said, "Why didn't you take care of that when he was unconscious so he wouldn't have to go through that pain again?"

The doctor said, "Oh, no, we could never let him stay unconscious."

In all honesty, I'd rather have stayed in the barn with my grandmother and come back after both toes had been done.

Growing up in a home where we were taught that death is a part of life has been a tremendous help in my adult life. Our family doesn't fear death. Death, for our family, is an event that can occur at any time. It's a relief of suffering and a spiritual justification for a life lived. Ma would say, "It's the only way out of this life."

Death was very much a part of the family. In Ma's day, the funeralization process occurred in the home. Seldom was anyone taken off to a nursing home or a hospital to die. They died in the home, were waked in the home or church, and the body was buried in the local cemetery.

Grandma was a stubborn individual. She didn't want her body to go to the funeral home at all. She insisted that she be "laid out" at home. The funeral director could come there and do the preparation work. She didn't go to his home when she was alive, why should she when she was dead? When she died, the funeral director came to the house and prepared her body in her bed. My mother and my aunt dressed her, styled her hair, and did her makeup. She was casketed in my aunt's home where she died and was taken to her own home for the wake and the funeral.

My aunt had been upstairs preparing herself to meet the neighbors who would be visiting that afternoon. Calling hours were all day, each day, until the burial. She came downstairs carrying a pitcher of water and, in passing, she glanced into the parlor. There was a man bent over my grandmother's body which was lying in repose in the bay window. My aunt turned and put the pitcher on the stand in the hallway. She proceeded into the parlor to greet the man who she assumed to be a neighbor. She turned around and the man was gone. She immediately went to the latched door and looked out the window. No one was walking down the walk. The man appeared suddenly and disappeared as rapidly.

A few weeks before she died, my aunt confided in me that she knew it was her father who had come to take her mother's spirit to heaven. He had died many years before. It gave her great comfort to know that he had come to take her mother to her eternal home. They were together again.

After she told me that story, she seemed comfortable in my reaction. My thirst for more stories led to another. It was after her father's funeral, in the early 1930s, that she had a very similar experience.

They lived in the rural farmhouse where Grandpa's wake and funeral were held. Preparing to retire for the evening, my Aunt Florence went outside to use the outhouse. It was a cold February night and the moonlight danced on the new fallen snow. She knew that it was light enough that she didn't need a lantern. She just left the door of the privy open. There were no concerns about anyone seeing her as the nearest neighbor was a mile down the road. Unexpectedly, she saw a man coming up the road, bent over in the cold. He had a heavy blanket over his shoulders and head and slowly walked up the driveway to the side door and went into the house. She thought it most peculiar but a kind act that the neighbor would come on that bitter cold evening to check on her and her mother, especially at that hour. She went into the house looking for the neighbor man.

Grandma said, "No one has come in here."

My aunt said, "Well, I just saw him walk up the driveway and come in the side door."

She ran to the door and opened it. The door was latched with a hook and there were no steps in the new fallen snow. It was then that she decided that Granddaddy had come home to check on his wife and children before he went on to his eternal rest.

This special aunt seemed to have a lot of spiritual experiences that affirmed her faith that we *do* live after the change called death.

As we sat reminiscing, my aunt told me about the footsteps on her stairs. The footsteps of a person going up and down the stairs. She wasn't quite sure who it was but she had a good idea. The footsteps had become more frequent in recent years and always in the night. Through the years the steps had gotten closer to the top of the stairs. She felt the footsteps were connected to her sister-in-law, a woman we called Aunt Kate.

Aunt Kate suffered from tuberculosis and could not care for herself. Her problems were probably more emotional than physical, but my aunt and uncle provided a home for her for thirty-nine years. She was my uncle's sister and he babied her as if she were a daughter. Aunt Kate worked a few days a week in her younger years, cleaning for a doctor. She never did more as her brother enabled her to live at his home basically for nothing.

My Aunt Florence and Kate were rivals for my uncle's affections. Aunt Florence experienced relief and freedom after Aunt Kate's death, but the steps on the stairs held her captive.

Several months prior to his death, my uncle had been hospitalized once again with a heart attack. I went to their home to be with my aunt. Upon arrival I found that she too had become ill. She had to be taken to the hospital with the onset of congestive heart failure. My uncle's condition was critical and my aunt was in unstable condition. I called my twin sister to come home. She was uncertain if she would come that night or the next morning. I told her to make the decision and let herself into our aunt's house when she arrived. "I'll be sleeping in the large guest room. You take Aunt Kate's room."

I was awakened at three in the morning as I heard Phyllis coming up the stairs. I yelled to her, "I'm in the big guest room. You sleep in Aunt Kate's room."

She didn't answer me, which I found odd. I reiterated, "I'm in the big guest room, you take Aunt Kate's room."

She still didn't answer. It startled me. I thought somebody else had gotten in the house. I could hear them coming closer and closer up the stairs. I went to the top of the stairs and saw a light gray cloud coming toward me. It got two steps from the top and went back down the stairs. I couldn't make out the identity of a man or a woman but it was of human size and shape.

The next day I told my aunt about it. She told me the footsteps were becoming more frequent and that when they reached the top, she or my uncle would no longer be with us. In July of 1979, when my uncle died, one of the first things my aunt told me was that the week prior, the steps had gotten to the top of the stairs.

It seems that footsteps on the stairs are not the only audio mysteries that have surrounded our family. There has been a superstition in the family for generations that when someone dies, they come back on the night of the funeral and knock at the door. When the door is answered no one is there. It is our loved one's way of saying good-bye.

My mother's first cousin was very close to her. On the night of my mother's funeral, Ruth and her husband Joe sat at their kitchen table. Three loud knocks sounded at the door. Joe went to the door. No one was there. Ruth said, "It must be Myrt letting us know she is leaving."

Joe, skeptically, insisted that he heard the knock, answered the door, and no one was there.

Several years later, I opened a funeral home in our small community. I resided upstairs at the funeral home. The downstairs was very elaborately done as a beautiful chapel. After much work, patience, and waiting, we received our first call. Actually, it was the man who had convinced me to go into the funeral business. Months earlier, when I had suggested the idea, he seconded the motion with constant encouragement.

Paul had a history of health problems but was stable with his health when he suggested the business venture in early summer. He was diagnosed terminally ill in September. Throughout the fall he checked the progress of the funeral home. In early November he called and asked me to visit him. During our conversation he advised me to work diligently as he would be our first call. I assured him he had a long time to live, but we both knew differently. We worked feverishly and within the month opened the funeral home.

Paul's condition worsened and, on a late December night, Paul died. When the call came I became overwhelmed with emotion. Paul was a man who had helped me all my life. He had helped many people. He was town justice and an all-around good friend. I remember being a paper boy and going into the restaurant where he ate every night after the death of his wife. He would sit me down with his daughter and buy me a meal. Though he was gruff, his acts of kindness certainly outweighed the toughness. The night he died I felt a loss but also the excitement he had instilled in me in establishing the funeral home.

My partner and I worked through the day to make sure everything was perfect. As Paul had said, his funeral was one of the biggest that our community had ever seen.

That night, as I lay in bed thinking about the funeral, I heard a noise at the door. Three loud knocks came from the brass door-knocker at the front entrance. I put on my robe and ran down the stairs. I thought it was a friend of mine who occasionally stopped by to chat. I swung the door open expecting to find my friend. All I saw was the snow sifting across the sidewalk in the winter winds. There were no footprints and no one in sight, just Paul saying good-bye with a thank you for a job well done. I wish I could have seen him to thank him for the many pats on the back that he had given me.

A person who was always there for me was there once again, knocking at the door.

CHAPTER ELEVEN

Dad's death should have been easy for me. After all, if I am honest with myself, it was an answer to my prayers. I prayed for years that God would find an answer to our family's tragedy. I fantasized that perhaps he would be killed in a car accident, have a heart attack or lung cancer, and the family might share a few years of respite from this tyranny. Then I would be consumed with guilt for days for daring to think such a thought, especially in the presence of God, let alone asking Him to lend an ear to such devious speculations.

Seven years after we buried our mother, Dad's alcoholism had worsened to the point where he was no longer caring for himself. His mental capabilities were rapidly reversing. We could no longer care for him at home.

We held a family meeting and consulted with a physician. The doctor suggested that we admit him to the hospital for a thorough examination. Dad had a growth on his back and the doctor suggested that we might use that as an excuse to get him to go into the hospital.

In early September, Phyllis, my twin, had come home to visit with Dad. She wasn't aware of how bad things were with her father as she lived about three hours away. Rick, my brother, was off to college and in his own world. Rose and I watched Dad's rapid decline. When Phyllis saw our father, unshaven, very thin, and scarcely knowing the world about him, reality stared her in the face.

She asked him if he had been eating. He insisted that he had. He said, "If you don't believe me, the sink is full of spiders." Phyllis didn't know that cast iron skillets were called spiders. She assumed that Dad had been eating spiders.

I enjoy that story. It reflects some of the only humor in a tragic situation.

The family decided to admit Dad to the hospital for observation. Phyllis was the only one that could possibly convince him to go to the hospital. After all, Phyllis was the only one Dad would obey in anything. We often begged Phyllis to persuade him to go to bed during his fits of drunken rage. Within minutes after asking he would get up and go to bed, mumbling that he would do anything for Phyllis.

After being hospitalized, Dad responded well. His mind was much clearer. He physically seemed better and on the path to recovery. The doctor met us and said there were some minor lesions of cancer in the liver, but the tumor on his back appeared to be benign.

I asked the doctor not to mention cancer to my father. Dad was very much a man and if he thought he had a disease that would render him helpless, it would consume him very rapidly. He would be dead within weeks.

The doctor informed me of his patient's right to know his condition and, besides, the cancer was so minute that his life expectancy would be another two to three years. The next day he told Dad.

Dad ceased to eat and he became lethargic. Ten days later he was in and out of a coma. Keeping with family tradition we sat death watch at the hospital. The vigil was twenty-four hours a day with someone from the family constantly at his side. The girls maintained vigil together and then I would sit with Dad. My brother would periodically pop in. Rick just couldn't handle the hospital scene so we didn't really expect him to be there.

A special time during that last couple of weeks was when my Aunt Helen came to be with me. She told me to rest on the bed next to Dad's bed. I did and fell asleep for hours. When I awakened we had a wonderful conversation about Dad and his brother Howard. She was Howard's widow. Unknowingly, she helped me to prepare for Dad's death, though I never really was fully prepared.

One afternoon I was alone with Dad. He had been in and out of consciousness for a couple of days. On this particular day he was scooched down in bed looking through the protective bars on the side of the bed. He saw me and called me by name. It was the first time he had been aware of who I was in probably two or three years. I was so excited that he recognized me. I hoped that he hadn't mistaken me for somebody else. He repeated my name. "Philip, you have to get me out of here."

I said, "Dad, you have to be in the hospital, you're not feeling well."

He said, "The hospital? I'm in jail. I know I'm in jail in Newark Valley."

He peered through the bars and I'm sure he thought he was in jail. Some of his past escapades took him so close to jail he was probably calling on the sins of the past with some punishment in the present. I lifted him up on the pillows where he could see he was in a hospital bed. His distress immediately subsided.

I sat with Dad and held his hand. He looked at me and said,

"Philip, why would you come and visit me after all I have done to you? All the pain and suffering that I've caused, why would you come and visit me?"

I welled up with emotion. My Adam's apple got at least three times its size. I wanted to say, "Dad, it's because I love you." But I couldn't. Instead, I said, "Dad . . . , it's because you're my Dad."

He looked at me. "Philip, I hope you can find forgiveness in your heart for all that I have done."

I wanted so bad to have a witness to these words but nobody, not even a nurse, was in sight. In the boldness of my rebellious adolescent self I looked him in the eyes and said, "Dad, you taught me to be an honest man. Right now I can't forgive you for all that you have done. How can I forgive you for a lifetime of hurt and pain? Someday, when I get where you're going, we'll sit down and talk things over, but right now I can't forgive you."

Within a short time Dad lapsed back into a coma.

I was sure Dad would die on the anniversary of Ma's death. We were rapidly approaching that day. His condition worsened. We were told that it would be, at most, any moment. The anniversary passed and Dad lived.

We were exhausted. My sister had to return to work or lose her job, my other sister had to return to her family, and I had a lecture on homicide investigation that I had looked forward to for months. I told my sisters that Dad was so close to death that he probably wouldn't know if we were there or not. We should go do what we had to do and I would check on him after my lecture. I did my lecture, how, I don't know, but I did. I left immediately afterward to check on Dad. I stopped at the sheriff's department and called the hospital. The nurse told me the end was very near and I should get there as fast as I could. He would die within the next two hours.

The intuitive feeling that one gets with the death of a loved one told me that I would be lucky to make it to the hospital before he died. I hastily drove there and ran from the parking lot to Dad's room. As I ran in his room a nurse grabbed me by the shoulder. "Philip, you didn't make it. He died about two minutes ago."

"God, no," was all I could say.

The attending nurse looked up, "No, he's not gone. He's still breathing."

I went to his bedside. With only a small table lamp lighting the scene, I held my father in my arms as his last breath left his body.

The nurse told me that he had quit breathing for about a minute and a half. She said, "I told him that you were coming, Philip. Suddenly he started breathing as if he was waiting for you to get here."

All I could say through my tears and my sorrow was, "I know, I know."

Once again, we found ourselves on a rainy late September weekend, planning a funeral. Seven years before it had been to bury our mother and this time to bury our father.

I needed to see Dad's body in repose. The only memory I had was of his frail, slender body in that hospital bed with his mouth open, lying back on the pillow in the dim light. I arranged to see Dad by myself. I needed to do that. I had things I needed to say.

A close friend of mine, Jim, went with me to the funeral home. There, in a casket similar to our mother's, lay the man I so desperately tried to love. The man I wanted to be proud of me. The man I wanted to hug me or pat me on the back. The man who could look at me and call me son.

I walked to the casket overwhelmed with grief. Jim, a quiet sort of guy, stayed back. He didn't know what to say or do. I knelt by the casket with the echo of my father's voice in my ear, "You can never be a son to me. You will never be a son to me."

I blessed myself in prayer. The years of argument, drunken abuse, and rage resounded in my head until it seemed to all run together.

I found myself apologizing to my father. "I'm sorry, Dad, that I could never be a son to you, but I tried the best way I knew how. I only wanted you to love me. I'm trying so hard to forgive you."

Soon other family members began arriving and I had to compose myself. I pretended nothing was wrong. Years of practice made me good at that.

The next day we buried Dad next to his mother. The burial was in a separate cemetery from where our mother was buried. I had promised Ma that she would not have to be next to Dad through eternity. She was buried between her mother and grandmother. There was a grave left next to Dad's mother, so we buried him there. Ma often said, "I hope I never have to say I've lived twenty-five years with that SOB."

She died two weeks before their twenty-fifth wedding anniversary. Now they were both gone and that chapter of my life was hopefully closed.

It wasn't. I carried the guilt of what I had said to my father that day in the hospital. Before I could forgive him he went into a coma and died. I just couldn't forgive him for all that he had done.

I talked to counselors and therapists. I needed relief from the guilt and grief I was carrying even several years after Dad's death.

I confided in a priest. He looked at me, his chin resting on his hand, a finger to the side of his mouth, intent upon the story.

He said, "You know, Phil, one of the most important things for your father was honesty. He needed to know he raised an honest son. In his death, you gave him that gift. You let him know that he had fulfilled himself with an honest son."

The burden of guilt and grief was lifted from me. I could continue with my life. I remembered the day of the funeral. I saw myself standing by Dad's grave as his friends folded the flag and Taps was played for his final farewell.

I looked on Dad with pride and love in my heart. Since then I have come to know that a good part of me is Dad—my quick wit, my humor, and my need to survive. The stubbornness, stamina, and strength of spirit that keeps me going is Dad. Everyday thoughts of Dad in anguish and bitterness are gone. I don't think of him so much any more. When I do, it's always with the fondness of a good story, the pride that he carried in himself, and the love that I have for him.

CHAPTER TWELVE

Fearful of sharing my secrets I have come to realize they are only thoughts. There is nothing powerful about them. Some people accept them, some arrange them to their own satisfaction, and some reject them. Though they may have changed some through the years they are still my thoughts. Thoughts that have been gathered together through the years of friendship with my talents. Talents I possess that have made me who I am. These talents have brought me some of the only self-confidence I have come to know in my life.

It is the fear of sharing these thoughts that makes me feel I am divulging the secrets of my soul. You see, there is no secret to my talent. There is only understanding of the world around me. I have been afraid of sharing these thoughts because of the socially-induced fear of rejection. Rejection has been an ever-present part of my world. Some of my thoughts may seem peculiar and beyond the grasp of reality. My hope is that others will find answers through my experiences.

I first became aware of the spirit world by visual contact with that unseen world. I tried to reject the experiences but came to the realization that it was a visualization of a world around me. A world I could not see but always knew existed. I couldn't always share my experiences with others because, in sharing, I would find great discomfort from the reaction of people I loved. Yet to those that I could share my experiences, I found a wonderfully intriguing pursuit of their spirit and the spirits that have gone before us. The events have been a validation of my faith and my faith has been a validation of my spirit. I now know the body is temporal and the spirit is eternal.

The first time I saw a spirit was during the summer of 1966, the year I became aware of my gifts. A group of friends and I were talking about spiritual things. We decided we would try a spiritual circle. In days of old, and before people got uptight with spiritual and religious philosophies, these spiritual circles were called "seances."

We placed a candle in the middle of the kitchen table. Five or six of us sat around the table holding hands. I had read about spirit circles and decided that I would be the medium, only because I had more knowledge of what was going on than anybody else at the table. We sat with our heads bowed and our eyes closed, probably more to keep from giggling than to communicate with the so-called spirit world. After a few moments the group became more serious, but there were still several outbursts of laughter and nervous giggling.

A few moments into the session I opened my eyes. I saw a man standing behind my friend, Rene. He was enveloped in a grayish-blue haze. The man was very pale and had thin sunken cheeks, a bushy mustache circling the corners of his mouth, and a full head of dark wavy hair.

He placed one hand on Rene's shoulder and said, "My name is John. I am her grandfather."

I closed my eyes very tightly as a child might having just seen a ghost. I guess because, literally, I *had* just seen a ghost. Everyone at the table sensed I had experienced a visualization and asked what I had seen. I described it to them.

Rene said, "My grandfather's name was John and he fits the description."

The next morning she showed me a picture of her grandfather. It was an exact image of the man I had seen in the spiritual circle. I found it exciting, puzzling, and disconcerting that I alone visualized Rene's grandfather. I was unaware the sight that was rapidly growing within my mind's eye was a special talent.

Our interest began to escalate. We traveled occasionally to a spiritualist camp not far from home. It was there that I had my first private consultation with a well-known medium.

I was young and I'm sure she thought I was doing this just for fun. She soon knew my interest in her work.

As the session began a mirror on the wall behind her began to go back and forth in a pendulum movement. She never said anything but I felt it was an indication of spirit presence as there was no source for the movement. She spoke to me in soft whispers.

"Your great-grandfather is here. His name is William Henry. He has a message for you," she said. "He doesn't know you, but recognizes you through descendancy of the family. He wants you to tell your mother that he went to Georgia prior to his death. He worked in the lumber industry and had an opportunity to go to South America. He took the opportunity and died there."

I found this story bizarre and knew it could not be true. If it were I would have heard it through tales in the family.

I shared the story with my mother. As I detailed the reading that I had been given she said, "We always wondered what happened to Grandpa. The last anyone saw him he was in a canoe headed down the Susquehanna River. His wife was throwing stones at him. They had a difficult relationship and he decided to take off. The family had received one letter from him, postmarked Georgia. He said in the letter that he was going to take a job in South America that would pay good money. Once his life improved he would come home and take care of the family. He never returned home and no one ever heard from him again."

What the medium had told me that day was apparently true. It was embarrassing for that generation of the family to share the conflict and failure of Great-grandpa. It was never shared with our generation. The information obtained was spiritual knowledge given to us so that we, on both sides of life, could establish spiritual peace from a situation that had obviously been spiritually distressing.

I have had thousands of spiritual experiences. Facts of identification from the spirit world have been made known to me and others with no doubt. It is comforting and peaceful to know that our loved ones are gathered on the other side with the same love that they shared when they were with us here on the earth plane.

Comfort and peace were never so present and significant as at the time I received the Sacrament of Ordination. It was the evening I became a minister of God in the non-denominational church.

The ordaining clergy placed their hands upon me and received me into the Order of Melchezidek, the Eternal Priesthood of ministers in the Christian faith. I closed my eyes in deep prayer, thanking God that he had placed my feet upon a path that had brought me to ordination. Although it wasn't exactly the ordination I had anticipated, it felt right and comfortable. There was a divine warmth that embraced me as I was ordained. I felt truly blessed. I opened my eyes and looked ahead. Standing before me was the Bishop who had confirmed many of the children from my childhood. He was the Bishop I would have wanted to confer the Sacrament of Ordination upon me, but, he had died several years before.

The Bishop held his arms outstretched with palms up in front of me. I looked at his face as it glowed with a special spiritual warmth. He looked at me and, with a depth of kindness that I've seldom known, said to me, "Philip, it is time to take up the stones that have been in your path and make them into a foundation for your church and ministry in the future."

The peace of that message brought forgiveness from within the depths of my soul. All the rejection and terror that the church had so freely given me in pursuit of Episcopal ordination didn't matter. It healed the open wounds immediately and took me into a state of grace, a grace that I needed for my new journey, and a grace that I needed to heal the wounds of the past.

I knew that I was meant to be a minister since I was seven. I was asked by the Bishop during the interview for seminary studies why I felt or knew that I was called to be a priest. The only answer I could give him, obviously unsatisfactory, was that I just knew. God told me that ordination was one of the gifts that I must share among His people and I always knew that the day of ordination would come. After all, doesn't love within the heart bring certainty that something is meant to be a part of your life? There may be times when we allow imagination to create a falsehood, but when something is truly a part of God's will for us, nothing can take that away from us and nothing can keep it from becoming fulfilled.

I have looked at the examples around me regarding talents, skills, careers, and the will of God as fulfilled in other people. Mother Theresa, for example, knew of her mission in life. I don't believe she focused so much on the mission that she did not busy herself with the work of the mission. The diligence and humility of her work created a truly great person. That greatness was born from the love of God within her. Mother Theresa became a channel for that love.

It is the burning desire within ourselves and the greatest gift of God's love for us that truly can change the world. If we could teach people peace within, that gift would radiate to the world from each person and we would have world peace. The peace of that love would cross all barriers and boundaries of race, creed, sexual orientation, and language barriers. It would travel to all ends of the earth to establish a peace within creation, the peace that God wants for us. The world can trace its unrest back to the unrest of individuals throughout the world. A fearfulness and a need for power that leads to the need to control. It is evident in my life and I believe it to be true for the world at large.

In my pursuit of the priesthood I found that love was drained from those essential to my mission and that their hearts were filled with fear by something that they did not understand.

The small rural church that had become my second home was filled with love. There were only traces of fear. It was simple—they knew me. People who did not know me began to be afraid of my psychic work. The fear seemed to intensify much faster than love. Think of the journeys taken in love, whether it be the love of another person, the love of a talent, the love of a hobby, or whatever the goal, that wonderful feeling that you can accomplish anything is ever-present in love. You know the fortitude and strength that you gain by that love.

Now recall some of your fearful moments and remember the doubts and uncertainties. How you fell faster and faster into fear in a spiritual free-fall where nothing felt certain. There was no goal or attraction. Just the emptiness of fear destroying whatever gets in its path. Anyone who has accomplished a mission in life will tell you that they have had to replace fear with love. There are no exceptions. The journey requires us to hurdle spiritual obstacles, people, and events cast in the path to strengthen our legs so as to continue the journey. It's not just people accomplished in life with notoriety or celebrity status. It's true of all people. No matter what class or walk of life, if you listen to the God within, you will find the mission. Even the greatest gifts can come in small packages wrapped differently than we may think.

I believed that I was to be an Episcopal priest. However, God's intent for me was to share myself spiritually as a minister in a non-denominational faith. He needed me in that role rather than the defined discipline and rigidity of the rules and regulations of the church. I needed to be free to share my spirit, not be told how to share my spirit or have it delegated by others.

I interviewed for the studies of the priesthood for three years. Batteries of psychological tests were administered as I pursued my vocation. My home parish was at a tender time for a rural church. I planned to be ordained so I could become a worker priest and continue my psychic vocation to support myself. The church could not afford to maintain a full-time priest. It would be exactly what the doctor ordered for both the church and myself. The three years of interviews and testing showed me the man-made quality of the church. The power and position people hold in the name of God is truly awesome to me. Although my involvement with the church in my early thirties was more rebellious than most, it created wonderful stories that I have carried with me since that awful time.

I traveled to a three-day career counseling retreat to receive intensive psychological testing. During that testing it was discovered that my relationship with my father was not the best. The psychologist said, "It did not seem the healthiest."

I wanted to look at him and say, "No kidding, Dick Tracy.

What primary school did you graduate from?" but I held my tongue. It was obvious the psychologist had grasped the opportunity to open the door for my eventual rejection if it were needed.

The Friday afternoon of the retreat was spent in psychological evaluation and Rorschach ink-blot tests. I allowed my imagination to run wild as I had been told to do. The counselor entered the room and commenced the evaluation.

Many people go into counseling because *they* need counseling. It appeared this man was no exception. He had dark, disheveled, oily hair. He wore plaid pants and a striped shirt. He must have purchased them with excitement in the late '60's or early '70's. His glasses were askew, their purpose seeming unfulfilled. His nose itched from allergies as he kept dabbing at it with a Kleenex, running his finger on the inside of the left nostril. I was uncomfortable being alone with him. What a wonderful sermon: "Cleanliness is next to Godliness."

We proceeded with our conversation. His nervousness intensified as the questions became more personal. Finally, he dared cross the threshold of inquiry into my sexual behavior. The topic has always been personal, as I trust it should be with everyone. It should be significant to me and my intimate partner. I am aware of the human interest that lies within us about everyone else's sexual appetites and behaviors. The church needed to know I was not a person who might betray society and the mores of the land.

A simple question or two would have sufficed. In nervous anticipation of the honesty with which I had answered all of his other queries, he began to pursue questions regarding my sexual preference, my previous sexual behavior, and my thoughts of future behavior. I was a single man in my early thirties. This made him uneasy and he needed that information, if not for the church, then for himself. He inquired about sex abuse. I answered him honestly in the negative. I assured him I had known since I was fourteen years old that, if I had gotten in a situation that I couldn't get myself out of, it was because I allowed myself to be in that situation. I never allowed anyone to force anything on me that I did not invite into my life, I was a responsible person.

He then approached the area of incest. He asked if there were any incestual incidents in my family. I assured him there were not. I had never seen my parents sleep together, not even in the same room. I wasn't even sure they had sex. Perhaps I truly was found under a cabbage plant in the garden, I speculated. He then casually mentioned, "There probably was no involvement with animals?" He moved quickly to the next question. I stopped him and, staring directly at him, brought him back to his inquiry.

I said, "I didn't hear that last question, would you mind repeating it?"

"Oh, I am sure there was no involvement with animals."

My stare intensified as I said to him, "Not since my German Shepherd died years ago." It was obvious through the stoic and determined look on my face and the horrified and mortified look on his that we had come to an understanding that these questions best come to an abrupt end, and they did. (By the way, we never owned a German Shepherd!)

Later that year I traveled to the church conference center for the final retreat. Soon I would be named to the Postulant (a person studying toward the priesthood). I was traveling the last seventy-five miles of a very long journey. I had come this far, I could continue across the finish line.

I reflected on an Ash Wednesday morning fifteen years earlier when I had gone to an Episcopal-affiliated college for an interview to become a student.

The childhood priest I idolized had attended that college. I foolishly thought if I could go to that college I could become just like him.

My aunt, uncle, and my mother traveled with me to the interview. We must have looked like Jed, Granny Clampett, and Jethro coming onto campus that day. The admissions committee scarcely took time to interview me. A student showed us around campus and it became certain I was not what they sought as a student. The admissions person assured me that I would probably go on and do wonderful things in my life, but quite frankly I was an average student. The review of my financial status was below their requirements. They were looking for someone that could ultimately benefit the college. Reference was made to financial endowment. I wanted to give him the twenty bucks that was folded in my pocket, but I planned to take my aunt, uncle, and mother out for lunch later that day. I chose to keep the money. Food in my stomach was better than sharing anything more with these people. My journey changed course.

All of the thoughts and daydreams of the past diminished as I approached the gates of the conference center. I came back to the present. I registered and was taken to the guest room. Interviews began within the hour.

During the interviews the Bishop asked me about my calling. The Commission on Ministry asked me what they thought were pertinent and justified questions. I did my best to elaborate in a way I thought could overcome the political maljustice that seemed so evident. It appeared that most of these people had made it to the top of the mountain and were fighting anyone who climbed up. I needed a unanimous vote from the Commission on Ministry in order to enter so I did my best to accommodate their needs.

Prior to leaving home I had received a call from my supervising priest. There was concern over my work in psychic phenomenon. The conflict originated with one priest. He lived thirty miles from my home parish. He was a man that, until my pursuit of the priesthood, I thought was open to my work. Twice I had lectured to his parish family. In the last lecture I had participated in the morning worship service. My supervising priest said to be cautious around this individual. He had a campaign in the Commission on Ministry to eliminate me from the worker/priest program. That afternoon I saw the priest talking with the church psychologist. Immediately the psychologist came to me and introduced himself. He wanted to take a short walk so he could get to know me. We walked toward the lake.

He told me he wanted to take this walk because we needed to be where no one else could hear what he had to say to me. He told me that he didn't believe in my work in psychic phenomenon and parapsychology. Although I had received celebrity status for my work, it was not valid. He would do anything in his power to see that I would never become a priest in the Episcopal church. Desperation came over me. If only someone else could hear what this man was saying. The priest from my past who had befriended me as I shared my gifts with his parish had become my Judas. At that moment my journey toward the priesthood had taken a sudden and dramatic turn.

The following week I received notification that I had six months to remove myself from the public eye regarding my psychic work. It was my income, but I had recently opened a restaurant. I decided that I would honor and respect their request, only earning money through the restaurant. I publicly announced in a newspaper article that the priesthood was more important than parapsychology and psychic phenomenon.

The next six months I busied myself in the restaurant and desperately tried to bury my psychic past. I was not true to God or to myself, I was true to the men of the church. The only thing accomplished was near bankruptcy.

They told me that in the September gathering of the Commission on Ministry it would be decided whether I could continue studies. The meeting was scheduled for two weeks after studies began so I would be allowed to begin my studies then. Five days before the Commission was to meet I received a call from my supervisory priest. It was a Monday evening. I was working in the restaurant. I picked up the phone and heard the familiar voice of Father Bill.

"I just wanted to see how you are doing since your rejection," he said.

I retorted with a bit of fear engulfing me, "The meeting isn't until this coming Friday. I don't have any results from their decision."

The priest who had become my Judas had called a special meeting. He had gotten four people from the Commission to vote against me. I could no longer pursue my path to the priesthood.

I felt as if somebody had reached into me with one hand ripping my guts out and with the other hand reaching up and pulling my heart out of my chest.

I thanked Father Bill for his love and ended the conversation as quickly as I could. My voice was quivering and my eyes filled with tears. I went to the kitchen, tears running down my face, purging my soul of all those years of anguish. I had come to a dead end or at least a stop sign.

God must have been prepared for this because my friend, Bill, stopped to visit. He was not a frequent visitor but I knew in Bill I had unconditional friendship. It was that friendship that saw me through those moments of despair.

My Judas was to have notified me of my rejection over the previous weekend. I never heard from him until two weeks later, when I received a brief note consoling me in my rejection. A note from the man who had accomplished his mission healed nothing.

I never heard from any of them again. I sought answers with letters to the Bishop, the Commission on Ministry, as well as various priests within the church. I was never told why I was unfit to be clothed as a clergyperson in the church. I became bitter. I had a lawyer pursue with a letter to the church but the only acknowledgment that came was that I had been rejected. That's the way it was and that's the way it would remain . . . never an answer.

I found it curious that the church, a spiritual organization that is supposed to lead you to the answers, had none. I am sure they feared a lawsuit or controversy, but I never received an answer from the family that I had found so many answers to throughout my life . . . to this day never an answer.

CHAPTER THIRTEEN

We cannot talk about the journey of the spirit without considering the idea of reincarnation. The belief that we may live more than one life has been believed as long as humans have had a spiritual philosophy or spiritual understanding. Through spiritual awareness we define our spirit with karmic knowledge assisting in the definition.

Earlier in my life I did not allow myself a belief in reincarnation. I was fearful it was not accepted by the church and it would be another mark against me. Since then I have learned that reincarnation was a belief common to the early church but was removed, perhaps because of the ideology of one or a few human beings in power at the time. However, the belief in reincarnation has continued in many different regions of the world and by many different cultures from generation to generation.

I began to acknowledge my belief in reincarnation when I heard a priest talk to a woman after church one day. He flippantly said to her, "Well, perhaps you did that in your last life." This statement came from a man who could never accept a belief in psychic awareness but yet his unconscious mind obviously had given some careful thought to it. Since that time I've acknowledged and accepted a belief in reincarnation.

It makes spiritual commonsense to me that we may not accomplish everything in one lifetime. We may get off the track of our spiritual journey or develop some karmic debt that needs to be repaid.

Karma, that spiritual entity that we seem to debit and credit to our life account, may pass from one life to another. Karma, in its true sense, is the fuel for spiritual progression. That progression is toward a nirvana or spiritual perfection. Therefore, if we seek perfection, we must work to eliminate imperfection. If we create negativity, we must harmonize bad with good as a step toward perfection. The eastern philosophies and religions of the world understand this. We, in the western world, have a tendency to point the finger and blame whatever our life's problem is on something or someone. We get stuck in the muck and mire of the past, neglecting the present and future.

I recall an incident in a psychic development class. Seven women gathered Saturday mornings for the class. One woman was gifted but quite obnoxious with her gift. Another woman was a kind woman, a registered nurse, who shared her feelings honestly. Personality conflicts arose concerning the friends and followers of each woman. I was friendly with the nurse, but, as well, found friendship with the other woman, although I was not quite as trusting of her. The first woman felt threatened and told me the group would be destroyed if I allowed the nurse to continue class. I assured her that the nurse was going to remain in the class. The woman tried, to no avail, to convince me that the nurse had personal designs on me. She was causing all kinds of problems. She supposedly had perceived all this psychically. I never perceived the nurse's personal interest in me, other than friendship. I would have been aware of that, had it been true.

The following week the first woman came in with a wonderfully preposterous story. She told me why she and her friends disliked the nurse. Supposedly, they had been together in a previous life. She, three friends, and the nurse were ancient astronauts who came to earth on a mission. There was conflict in their ranks and the nurse had destroyed the other four women in their spaceship before it left earth.

I shook my head in disbelief. I found it interesting that this woman fabricated this story. Although I had a belief in U.F.O.s, it was obvious this woman was using my beliefs as a ploy to get the nurse out of my class.

I spoke with her, "That may be true, I can't say. What we must do is embrace the opportunity and heal your karma by forgiving this woman for what she has done to you and your three friends in a past life. Through that forgiveness you can help her to overcome the negative karma created in the sabotage of your spaceship."

I never saw her or her three friends again. Their pursuit over karmic cosmic sabotage ended.

Often, people that are regressed go into their unconscious mind to perceive a past life. They will generally perceive a life of greatness, a life as a celebrated personality or someone who carried a wonderful talent. Regression of spiritual stature is a bit backwards from its karmic point of view. Perhaps it is part of our wants and desires to be somebody that we aren't and never will be. Obtaining information about reincarnation must be carefully done. There are many people willing to take your money for regressive hypnosis, for soul searching, or past-life involvement, who may not have the abilities to do so. I was regressed by a professional hypnotist and found the information concerning past lives to be helpful and informative. However, I must live my present life to the best of my ability, gleaning knowledge from the past. I discovered I had been a blacksmith in Virginia prior to the Civil War. I died in a fire in my home trying to save my wife. I had been working in my smithy shop in the early morning hours. I returned to the house to read a paper by lamplight. After finishing, I went back to the smithy shop and the lamp caught the paper on fire. The house burned before I could get in to save my wife. Early in my present life I had an extreme fascination with horses and blacksmithing. I have all the tools that my grandfather used for his own blacksmithing. The interest was beyond normal for a young child. I think I gathered that interest from another life.

As I work with people in past-life readings we often go back from whence we came. I visited Ireland for my first time and knew I had lived in the area of Galway in a previous life. I could find my way around, even in contemporary times, from knowledge of a past life. Often we see interests, likes, and dislikes that may be associated with a past life. We reflect upon them with acceptance or rejection because of our karmic condition. Remember one thing—if you drown in a past life you best learn to swim in the present life. Learn to love the water you hated and you will overcome your karma and realize your spiritual perfection without having to travel through many more lives.

At one time or another we have all had the experience that we have previously experienced an event or situation. That uncanny feeling where you know what is happening as it happens or you know what is going to happen next. The experience is commonly referred to as *déjà vu*. It is that discovery that suggests to all people that they may have some psychic capabilities or precognitive experience. It is this mental phenomenon connected to the unconscious part of the mind that allows us to know that our mind is continuously recording information from the past, present, and future. Our minds scan the world around us for information, protection, preservation, and awareness.

Our conscious mind decides what information will be revealed to us. Some information will remain sealed in the depths of the unconscious mind. This information that is stored may periodically be revealed to us in a thought that suddenly surfaces, a dream, a precognitive experience, or as *déjà vu*.

Unwittingly, information may be recorded and stored in the unconscious mind about an event that lies ahead. As we approach that event, the fact that we are living the foreseen experience triggers the memory bank to bring the stored information to conscious awareness, cued from the familiarity of the event. The unconscious mind passes the information to conscious awareness and we have an instant replay going on at the same time the event is occurring. Thus, it gives us the feeling that we have been there before. In actuality, we *have* been there before, in the mental processes and the in-depth reaches of our mind.

We can be so familiar with the event as it happens that we may know moments ahead what is going to be said or what the outcome shall be. The *déjà vu* attachment creates the psychic event.

When we fully learn the process of *déjà vu* we shall find "comfort in knowing" as events occur. We will know when that experience begins whether it is going to end in a positive or negative way and be able to respond accordingly. The knowledge will save us aggravation, humiliation, and not jeopardize our life in any way. We will come to understand precognition (knowledge of events beforehand) is a part of the natural workings of the human mind. *Déjà vu* is closely connected to instinct, the need to survive to fulfill the purpose of our creation.

When we understand *déjà vu* we will know that the unconscious mind works continuously for our benefit, whether waking or sleeping. Information is continuously being stored in the unconscious mind and the conscious mind may call upon that reserve at any time. Whether it be a foreboding, an elation, a dream, or *déjà vu*, we will know that the impressions received and stored in the unconscious mind are all part of the human experience. Nothing will be mysterious and no one will be fearful of an unknown element. It will be regarded merely as the unconscious awareness instinctively trying to exist in a conscious world.

We will rely on the power of our dreams as merely another extension of ourselves. A source of answers to life's questions. We will look at the unseen world around us with commonsense, knowing that our world is not contained just within our flesh and bones or within the material world in which we exist. We will understand the mind perceives much more than we may believe it to perceive. We will no longer live in a dream world but in a world where dreams are reality.

Everything that is created began with an idea, a mental process that was ignited by the fires of passion for life to become reality. We, as humans, will go on to know that we must go to the depths of our souls to find the answers to questions that may have only scratched the surface to the meaning of the universe and our role in it.

CHAPTER FOURTEEN

The aura is an energy field that surrounds all living things, both plant and animal. Sensitives are able to see the aura and interpret its colors and activity to the life processes. I had read about the aura but had never seen one until June of 1973. I probably had never seen an aura because I was trying too hard consciously. So intent, in fact, that I was unable to go into my unconscious mind and create the mental conditions necessary for seeing the human aura.

My first visualization of the human aura came during church one Sunday morning in 1973. The Bishop of the diocese was visiting to administer the sacrament of Confirmation. The prayer of consecration prior to Holy Communion is probably one of the most spiritual moments in worship. The consecration prayers create the ultimate definition of our being, bringing together earthly imperfections and heavenly aspirations into a perfect communion. The prayers grant forgiveness for things done and left undone and allow hope for a better life. During these meditative prayers our minds will often transcend into our unconscious thoughts. It is there that we can deal with the events of life, all the shortcomings

117

and misgivings. It is there we prepare for anything the world may offer us.

This particular Sunday morning I was involved in an exceptional spiritual and meditative experience. I gazed upon the cross during the prayers of consecration, reminding me of the suffering that had already been done for me, bringing the hope of the resurrection. My eyes left the cross and I glanced at the Bishop. His arms were outstretched, involved in the prayers of consecration where the bread and wine become for us the body and blood of Christ. He was mystically engulfed in a radiant purple light with white and silver throughout. I looked away as I thought the sunlight through the stained-glass windows might be playing tricks on me. I thought I was succumbing to a deeply spiritual event or perhaps the heat of the warm summer morning was rendering me unconscious. I rubbed my eyes and looked again. The energy was still surrounding the Bishop. The more involved the prayer became, the more intense the colors of light. I knew I had seen the aura.

Since then I have been able to go into the appropriate mental state to be able to see the aura at will. At first I had to look away from the person and then look back, look away, and then look back, and eventually the aura would appear. The more frequently I tuned in to seeing the aura, the more readily I was able to see it, so that now I see the aura merely as second-nature sight. It is as visible as anyone's limbs, eyes, or hair. Through years of association I have developed a means of interpretation which gives me a general definition of the aura. I then psychically investigate the aura for a more accurate definition of the person's personality, physical, and psychological makeup.

The ability to read auras has satisfied not only a psychic quest, but also satisfies a natural curiosity present in most people. It helps me in my daily life. I read people's auras to know what they think about me, to develop a commitment of trust, and to know when a person is lying. It helps me to know if they are sincere and physically well.

One day, shortly after I started reading auras, I noticed an unusual color across the left side of a woman's left breast. I mentioned to her daughter that I felt there was a problem that could either be cancerous or lead to a cancerous condition. The daughter said her mother had just had an exam about two months before and that everything was fine. I encouraged her to have the doctor check it more closely in the next exam. I apparently instilled some fear because she took her mother for a checkup immediately. The doctor found a small lesion that was removed without incident. The lesion had been overlooked because of its minute nature in the earlier exam.

I have also read auras of people who are comatose. I was asked by a family to examine a young comatose woman's aura to see what I could perceive about her mental and physical well-being. She had been in a coma for several years from injuries sustained in an automobile accident.

I went to the hospital posing as a friend of the family as the doctors working with her were not accepting of psychics working in the hospital. While I was reading her aura the doctor came in and we were introduced. He recognized my name and although he seemed reserved, he was interested in what I had to offer. With no beforehand knowledge I told him the location of the injury which had occurred many years prior. I was exactly right. I told him there was a bright haze of red around the left kidney and either she had a kidney infection or was passing a kidney stone. I felt strongly that it was a kidney stone. He told me many comatose people have kidney problems but there had been no signs of kidney infection. During my visit the next day, the doctor told me that his interest in my work had intensified. During the night the young woman had passed a kidney stone.

Many times the aura is affected because of psychological influences. There is no awareness that our body and mind are influencing the colors of the aura.

Several years ago, one New Year's Eve, I attended a party in the home of some very close friends. It was the usual New Year's Eve party, people bringing goodies and refreshments, gathering for conversation, music, and dance.

Around ten o'clock that evening I noticed the daughter-in-law of the hostess had a sudden and dramatic change in the color of her aura. I inquired if she had experienced a death in the family. The colors of the aura, to my interpretation, meant that she had gone through an incredible loss, yet no one could verify her loss. As the night continued her mood changed from her jovial, happy self to a more sullen introversion. The party continued, New Year's came and went, and I went home.

Early the next morning I was awakened by a phone call. The woman whose aura had changed so abruptly had received word that her brother had been killed in a car accident. His car had plummeted over an embankment into a gully and he was not found until the next morning. The investigation proved the accident occurred around ten o'clock the previous night, the precise time the woman's aura changed.

The bond of connection we call love made her aware of her tragic loss before the news reached her conscious mind.

Many such occurrences are connected with the aura. A pregnancy may be evidenced in a woman's aura because her body knows it before her mind. Disease or frustrations to a certain area of the body become obvious in the aura because the body becomes aware of it first and passes it to the conscious mind. The unconscious mind is constantly perceiving and changing the colors of the aura.

Through my work as an ambulance attendant and minister, I have watched as people die and their aura dissipates from their body, rising in spirals of energy above the dying body. Even after death there is a thin aura around the body which I attribute to some of the living organisms and bacteria that still may be contained in that body, doing their work toward decomposition. The aura is very shallow and insignificant in color. Life, as that person knew it in the body, has ended.

People who have been suffering will often have an improved aura just prior to death. I often think they're getting better. Actually they are in transition into the next life. They have overcome the suffering of their present body and its present condition. They have accepted a spiritual transition into another life. Their aura is improved because spiritually and physically they have made it through the death experience. It shows their earthly suffering has ended and their heavenly journey has begun.

I stumbled on the aura dissipating from the body in death quite by accident.

Early in my police work I was called to the scene of a drowning. A man had been swimming with a friend in a spring-fed farm pond and disappeared. He called for help and went underwater, never to be seen again. His friend searched in vain. Emergency personnel were called to the scene. After the initial investigation, I was radioed to report to the scene to assist. At the scene, Dave, head of the underwater search team, approached me and asked me if I knew the location of the individual. It was a large pond with deep dark waters. The evening hours approached and natural light was minimal. Dave wondered if the drowning had actually taken place or if somebody might be perpetrating a missing person case for some unknown reason.

I looked out across the pond. I could see energy coming out of the water and dissipating into the air in a small three-foot area across the center of the pond. I instructed Dave to go to that area and dive. He took his snorkel, swam quickly to the area, and went under. He came up and immediately went back down. He surfaced again clutching the body of the drowned man.

A short time later I was called to another drowning. A man and a young girl had drowned in the river. I responded to the scene. The sergeant and many water search-and-rescue personnel were there. I was asked my opinion concerning the location of the bodies.

I walked across a bridge near the area of the tragedy. I could once again see energy dissipating from the water. I suggested they check there. The rescue personnel arranged for a search boat because I wanted to check the area for myself.

An older man in charge of the search told me that my work was foolishness. He claimed he knew the bottom of the river, as he had lived by the river his entire life. He said it was not possible for a body to be where I indicated. I suggested to him that high waters and the constant churning of the river might change the bottom each year. He insisted that it did not.

I told him my impressions that the smaller of the two individuals would be found where I had said.

"It will be tomorrow morning at ten o'clock," I assured him. At 10:04 a.m., the girl's body surfaced exactly where I had indicated. Unfortunately, I'm not always successful in my searches. The man's body was not found for several weeks and about ten miles further downstream. Perhaps his body, being heavier, had stayed in the current longer and was away from the area before I arrived. In honesty, there are just times that it doesn't work for me.

Another search in the Finger Lakes of New York state was for a young girl who had drowned. I felt that she was in an inlet near the end of a boat. I could see she had fallen in, hit her head, and was rendered unconscious, drowning before she regained consciousness. A city police officer, who respected my work, brought me into the case. He wanted to search the inlet but others assumed her to be kidnapped or that she had wandered off. Investigators brought in search dogs and followed their leads. The dogs wandered everywhere the little girl had gone in her day of play prior to her death. Her body was found the next morning at the end of the boatslip in the inlet. There was a wound to her forehead where she obviously had bumped her head, became unconscious, and drowned.

Not everything I see is connected with the human aura, especially in my searches. I open my abilities to all my senses in an extrasensory way.

Another case was in the same community of the inlet drowning. My accuracy in that situation led the investigating officer to believe I should be involved in a double missing persons case.

A young man had fallen into a gorge on an ice-covered trail. A would-be rescuer slid on the same ice and went into the raging waters. Both men disappeared within seconds in the spring runoff. The lieutenant of the Park Police asked if I had any psychic impressions on the missing persons.

A woman co-worker of the rescuer brought me a map of the gorge and I "X'd" three places on the map. I felt they would find the body of one victim under one "X" and in the location of the other two "X"s they would find evidence to conclude the men had definitely drowned. I told them, in the course of my reading, that they would find a red flower above the area in which one of the bodies would be found. I emphasized they should keep up their search in the gorge.

The usual conflict of believer versus disbeliever and agency versus agency had to be handled. One investigation agency felt they had searched the gorge three times and should focus on the inlet leading into the lake just beyond the gorge.

A young officer who had faith and confidence in my work raised enough hell that they searched the gorge again.

They resumed the search of the gorge. Under one "X" they found the sneaker of one of the individuals. Under the other "X" they found the wallet of another of the missing persons. Mysteriously, under the third "X", caught in a tree across the waters, were flowers, red flowers, from a prayer vigil that had been held on a bridge upstream a couple of nights before. Under the log was the body of the rescuer. Clinging to the tree above was the red flower.

Not all searches end in success, but many of them have helped with evidence in a case, and I am satisfied with my investigative skills.

It's unfortunate that other psychics have given bad publicity to psychic involvement in police work and that investigative agencies are not open to the use of a reputable psychic. Psychic clues may answer questions concerning a disappearance or a death and renew commitment of investigators to a case. It's frustrating that harmony cannot come for police and psychics to work together.

Daily, people ask me to read auras. The general public, the medical profession, and law enforcement agencies are all intrigued by this phenomenon. Through the years, my acquaintance with people in the forensic science field has led to my being asked to consider cases and prepare reports. I have been asked to consult on the jury selection for homicide trials as well as observe interviews and line-up procedures. I am generally asked by the defense attorney. Why? My theory is: with my assistance, perhaps we can uncover hidden things about a potential jurist that could make the trial more fair and impartial to the defendant. Jurors may have an ax to grind, may be physically incapacitated, or may be emotionally frustrated so that sitting through trial eight hours a day would be difficult. In the jury selection process the attorneys become very involved in picking the best possible jurors with consideration for not just who might be best for a particular side but who might be fair, impartial, and neutral, thus obtaining justice for all.

Years ago I had occasion to be involved in the trial of a young man accused of murder. I was able to glean information that was helpful to the case, although evidence convicted him before the trial began.

In the early '80s I sat in on the jury selection for Jean Harris, the scorned lover of Dr. Herman Tarnower, the Scarsdale diet doctor. Ms. Harris had been charged with murdering him in a fit of rage, inflicting repeated gunshot wounds.

Dr. Tarnower had developed a new relationship with a younger woman. Jean Harris, a reputable teacher at a private girl's school, had traveled several hours to confront him. She discovered the younger woman, whom she thought had left his life, had been at his home. Through this discovery and the rage that ensued, gunshots were fired and Dr. Tarnower lay dead with Jean Harris accused of his murder.

My involvement began at a lecture on homicide investigation concerning the use of psychics and hypnotists in police investigation. A forensic scientist, well-respected in bloodstain evidence, approached me and pressed the casing of a bullet in my hand. It was obviously from a small caliber gun. He prompted my impressions concerning the bullet. Unaware of the case, I gave my impressions as I held the casing.

"I feel that the person who pulled the trigger of the gun that fired this projectile was a woman. She was a very jealous woman.

She was a very enraged and distraught woman, going through great emotional distress to the end that her emotions precipitated the crime."

"Can you tell me anything about anyone else involved in the crime?" he asked.

"I feel that the projectile from this bullet resulted in injury and death to a man who wore a white coat in his work, a doctor, I would presume," I continued.

The forensic specialist was so impressed that he contacted the attorney for the defense. The attorney called me in to be involved with the jury selection. I spent several days in White Plains, New York, for jury selection.

The trial was interesting for me as we kept my identity secret. The first moments of opening day I shook hands with the judge as I was introduced by the defense attorney. He told the judge that I was a psychic and parapsychologist who would be assisting in jury selection. The judge, busy in thought, never mentally registered what he was told. Later, it appeared he had no knowledge of my profession.

Of course, the media was interested in knowing my identity. After all, it was one of the most sensational cases in the country. Cameras were not allowed in the courtroom but the media trailed us and snapped our pictures frequently. In the courtroom I was the subject of sketches that appeared on the national network news. Soon my identity became a matter of concern for the prosecution. Who was this unknown person? On one occasion I came in from the midday lunch recess and noticed an assistant to the District Attorney looking at the name tag on my briefcase. Normally I would have been upset over this infringement on my privacy. However, the night before I psychically knew this was going to happen, so I left a fictitious name and address of a person in

Texas on my briefcase I.D. tag. I wonder how long they spent trying to track that person down!

Jury selection went well. I knew there were a couple of individuals that would be difficult, but for the most part I was satisfied.

I passed on my psychic impressions to the defense attorney. I discovered that one person had had back surgery two months previous and would not be able to sit through trial. I discovered another person found difficulty in dealing with death. She had lost a two-year-old grandchild within a few weeks prior to jury selection. This juror proved to be an interesting subject in the jury selection. The defense attorney asked her in *voir dire* if she had any trouble with the concept of death. I had told him that she was a good juror but was having difficulty handling death through the death of someone close to her. She began to sob and asked to have private *voir dire* in the judge's chambers. In chambers the defense attorney once again asked her if she had trouble dealing with death. He said he understood that she had recently lost somebody close to her. She sobbed as she came to the admission that her granddaughter had died and death certainly was fresh in her mind.

The prosecution stood up and asked how the defense attorney knew that information. The judge chimed in, "And how did you know that?"

The defense attorney calmly said, "Just conjecture on my part, your honor."

The prosecution attempted, through the channels of the courtroom, to discover my identity, but I maintained an incognito status throughout the trial.

My duties were coming to an end and we were rapidly approaching trial. One day at lunch I mentioned to the defense attorney and the forensic scientist that I thought Jean Harris stood a good chance of winning if, and only if, she did not take the stand in her own defense. I noticed as people watched her that their aura changed in color and activity. They felt she considered herself better than anyone and that she carried herself in a way that did not seem remorseful. I knew if she took the stand she would be convicted.

A few weeks later, as the trial ended, Jean Harris took the stand in her own defense. The jury deliberated and reached a verdict—guilty of murder. Jean Harris served several years of her sentence and was later released.

Many people in the world become so frazzled from the emotional peaks and valleys of a relationship that they are consumed by that relationship. Jean Harris was no exception. Many of us have been to the point of emotionally breaking, where a sudden wrong move may change our lives forever, a "There but for the grace of God go I" situation. The trial was one of the most significant events in my life. It helped me to know and understand my own actions in the scope of human behavior and that I should never allow anyone to rob me of my own spirit, not even myself.

I was also involved in jury selection for the Waneta Hoyt case, a woman in Tioga County, New York, who was accused of suffocating her five children some twenty-five years ago. The death of Waneta's children had been ruled as crib death or Sudden Infant Death Syndrome.

A prominent doctor in the Syracuse, New York, area had studied the family and concluded that the children's deaths were attributed to SIDS and that it was a probable genetic connection with multiple deaths in the same family. Years later, another doctor refuted the studies and findings of the original doctor. A medical battle ensued and the District Attorney brought charges of murder against Waneta Hoyt. This was one of the most tragic and

distressing cases I ever became involved in. I cannot offer com-
ment, as my thoughts about the case are still being reviewed in
my own psyche. I do know that I still pray for both sides. Issues
regarding the case seem unresolved even after trial. She was convicted—guilty as charged. It was a case where everyone chose a
side and often would ping-pong back and forth between sides.
The general public still seems undecided and although people
have taken some definite stands, there is a real sense of tragedy,
laced with uncertainty, all the way around.

CHAPTER FIFTEEN

I have worked with the human aura for many years and can discern whether healing is taking place or whether there is still disturbance, whether the mind and body have come together in communion to establish a more perfect being, or if there is still disintegration of the body and mind union.

The energy field of one person can mingle with the energy field of a sick person to give enough strength for healing to occur. The bond of love and healing assists the energies of the sick person so that they may be strengthened enough to overcome their infirmity.

There are many spiritual consequences which are important for healing to take place, but basically it is the harmonizing of the energy fields that creates a healing within the individual.

Healing may be spontaneous due to a spiritual or emotional event. It may be in the trust and confidence of modern medicine or, in spiritual awareness and recognition that someone has healing abilities, that our trust in them prompts healing. All healing must come from within. We touch the God force with an understanding that we must be healed to maintain a quality of life to fulfill our purpose for being here. If we look at all the great healers in the world, from Christ through Catherine Kuhlmann to Edgar Cayce to the gurus of eastern philosophies, we find the basic elements of love, trust, and harmony have enveloped a negative force and replaced it with positive healing energy. The incidences of healing that I have seen in my life have occurred in such an atmosphere. There is always the element of divine intervention that seem to suddenly come in and make a bad situation better.

Communion with our creator is often the impetus for healing. The realization that our work on earth is not yet accomplished and a need to continue our work in most favorable conditions often creates the atmosphere for healing. Only two people will know when our work on earth is done—ourselves and our creator. Others may beckon us to stay, or we ourselves may decide to leave, whichever, death is a decision between God and ourselves. We often forget that our physical body is a temple for God to dwell in while we are here. We abuse and destroy that temple or things may come into that temple that ultimately destroy it. We, the spirit of God as contained in our personality, will not move from that temple until everything has been fulfilled. Like karma, the fulfillment of our spirit being here may not be solely for our spiritual benefit but also for the benefit of those around us.

Several times I have journeyed with the spirits of others contained in a sick or injured body. I have touched their spirit in a special way so that they themselves could decide that their mission in life had not been fully accomplished. Though I may have opened the door to healing or a temporarily improved quality of life, it was their searching spirit that allowed the healing to take place. Their spirit remained in its essential position in creation blessed by the approval of God.

Years ago I was called to the bedside of my godson's grandmother. She was in her early eighties and in failing health. She was not baptized and her family asked me if I would administer the sacrament of Baptism. As I approached the waiting room of the hospital I could see about thirty people. Her family had gathered because of their love for this woman. Grandma had thirteen children and each of them had several children, so trailing her through life were well over a hundred children, grandchildren, great-grandchildren, and even great-great-grandchildren. They all respected and loved her as the matriarch of the family. They all wanted her to live but, if she couldn't, they wanted her baptized to receive the blessing of God for a safe and secure journey to her heavenly home.

The doctors said she was in the final two hours of her life. I hastily went to the hospital to administer Baptism. Our spirit should be aware of the sacrament of Baptism while we are still in the body. I offered the usual prayers and administered the waters of Baptism as she lay in a coma. Her death seemed imminent so I stayed with the family. The first hour passed. We tried to make small talk to wiile away the time. Each time the door opened we were certain the news of her death awaited. Precisely at the point of two hours she opened her eyes. She was weak and could not speak but as time went on she gathered strength and improvement became obvious.

She was alive for six more years, sharing in the love of her family in births, weddings, Christmas, all the holidays and special times that create the memories of a family, as well as family sorrows during that time.

The decision she made, in the presence of God, was that she was still needed and wanted on earth. She had missions to accomplish to fulfill her spirit. The sacrament of Baptism administered at the time of her decision helped her to realize that her life was not over.

More recently, I was called to the hospital to do prayers for my cousins' mother. She was in her eighties and had gone through life bearing the struggles of any large family. She had lost a young child due to an epidemic, another child was institutionalized for brain tumors, and she had lost a couple of children at young ages to premature and untimely deaths. She was an inspiration, for even in the face of adversity and disenchantment she was able to replenish her strength through the love that surrounded her. Earlier, she had open heart surgery and although her health periodically declined, she would regain strength and continue with her life.

I stood at her bedside with three of her daughters sitting around the bed. The daughter instrumental to her care for the past several years was sitting beside her. She was obviously distressed. Another daughter whispered to me that her mother had been in a deep sleep since four o'clock the previous afternoon. The medical staff indicated it was a comatose condition that would worsen and lead to her death. I hinted to her family that it might be time for her to be done with this life, that her age and her periodic decline may be seeking that ultimate rest. Her daughter, the "worry person" for the family, looked at me with sorrowful eyes.

"I really just want to talk to her one more time," she said. "I have things I still need to say to her."

I began the prayers. I whispered in the sleeping woman's ear. They were audible whispers because the woman was nearly deaf.

"Kate, open your eyes and talk with us. People here have things they need to say."

I continued with prayers for healing and ended with the Lord's Prayer. I finished and Kate opened her eyes.

She said, "Philip, what are you doing here? I must have dozed off." She had not realized she had been sleeping for sixteen hours.

The elements of healing harmonized. The needs of her family and her own spirit were mingled and Kate proceeded to get better.

Today, she continues to walk with the love and devotion of a mother and the head of her family.

A couple months later a member of my church had fallen critically ill and lapsed into a coma. He was in the intensive care unit at the hospital. Ted was a wonderful friend, always there spiritually with a wonderful love and support to our parish family. His family called me to his bedside. I walked into the intensive care unit, finding his granddaughter sitting beside his bed, holding his hand. She was studying for her finals in a chiropractic college.

Ted's vitals were severely suppressed and death was expected at any minute. I asked his granddaughter's permission to do prayers with him. She held his hand and mine and I held her hand and his as we did the prayers in a small prayer circle. I ended by holding his hand and placing my other hand on his forehead, asking God to bring him peace as quickly as possible. After the "Amens," I was talking with his granddaughter, preparing myself for final farewells to my friend. The nurse popped into the room. She checked the monitors and said, "Oh, my, I guess we should get you to work here in the intensive care unit."

"Oh, why is that?" I asked.

She said, "Ted's vitals are perfectly normal right now. They haven't been this good since he was brought into the hospital. You must have a wonderful healing touch."

I felt terrific. I was sure Ted knew I was there and I was able to bring peace into his tormented body. However, early the next morning, Ted chose to leave that suffering body and died.

Love and prayers are one of the most integral elements in healing. Whether for humankind or others in the animal kingdom, there is a real need to know that we are loved and needed. Through thoughts, prayerful meditations, and other acts of kind-

ness and love the elements of healing gather together and harmonize and make a difficult situation better.

Molly has been my dog and best friend for fifteen years. She
knows all the secrets of my heart and has never once feigned her
unconditional love for me. Even in my most angry and tempera-
mental moments she is always there with a nudge that lets me
know everything will be okay, and even if it isn't, she'll be there
with me. Molly is a black lab and basset mix. She has the appearance of a black lab on basset legs wearing a tuxedo. A little
white shirt in front, a long snout and long ears, and short legs
make for a sight to behold. She has a mind of her own, probably
because her master spoils her. She does anything she wants. If
there is trouble to be found, it's probably while foraging for food.
She eats continuously at the hand of her master.

One morning, as I was playing with Molly on the floor, her
lip came back and I noticed a rather large growth on the right
side of her upper jaw. I immediately knew it was bad news. I took
her to the veterinarian and after examination he indicated that it
must be removed and I should prepare for the worst. The tumor
in all likelihood was a melanoma cancer. Uncontrollable tears
streamed down my face as we journeyed home. I knew her fate
was not good. Molly moved closer to me in my distress as if to
say "Everything will be fine, Dad."

Four days later, with a heavy heart, I took her for surgery. I
prayed for everything to be okay but surgery proved otherwise.
It verified the growth to be a melanoma tumor. The veterinarian
removed it along with part of the jawbone and a tooth. He said
it was a vicious type of cancer and would probably return. She
would be dead within four months.

I was so thankful we would have four months together that I

was quite elated. At least I didn't have to make the decision to end her life that day. I took Molly home in her weathered condition. She was battered from anesthesia and the rigors of surgery. She was rather punky for a few days. I gave her soft food which she declined. The end was fast approaching. We spent many tearful hours in melancholy reminiscence about our years together.

Then one morning I decided that I should be doing prayers with her. I put her in a self-created hospice program. I had seen it work for people and Molly was every bit a person as anyone else in my life.

Molly loved all foods, especially boneless, skinless chicken breasts and sirloin burgers. I went to the wholesale outlet and got several packages of chicken breast and sirloin burgers for her hospice meals. I specially prepared each meal. Soon Molly's appetite returned.

Three or four months passed and she was subdued. Suddenly I could see her spirit return and her eyes, fading into the darkness of death, suddenly had new life. Each day I did prayers and gave her a total body massage. The love from my heart conveyed through my hands was helping her (along with the sirloin burgers and chicken breasts!). I watched for the tumor to return but apparently the high protein diet and my love restored her to newness of life. Today she is as much Molly as she was sixteen years ago. Although she was given three or four months to live, it has now been a year and a half. Her health is better today than it was for the two or three years prior to her illness.

I trust in the technology of modern medicine and hold in high regard my faith and divine interventions for the power of healing. Molly and God, along with a little nudging from Phil, decided it wasn't time for her to go to doggie heaven. Since that time we've had lots of time to talk and we know that the day will come when we part. We're both ready for that now and when it does happen, it happens. We know that the day will come when our eyes will come together in a communion of certainty that today is the day. There will be tears of sorrow and sadness, but we will both be thankful for the life we had together and the days that we share one day at a time.

AFTERWORD

Dear Dad,

I just got home from the movies. My friend Bill and I saw Stephen Spielberg's movie "Saving Private Ryan." It's a movie about the D-Day invasion of Normandy on June 6, 1944. It's a story related to the specific battle at Omaha Beach, the exact spot you entered the war in Europe. You would have been proud of me, I remembered the names of all the towns you were in and most everything regarding the campaign.

The movie was frightfully realistic. I know it sounds dumb, but I kept looking for you through the whole movie. Several times I saw people I thought could have been you and in my heart I knew it had to be you. I remember the night terrors and fears that you lived with after the war for the rest of your life. I remember you told us never to wake you from a sound sleep as you would come up fighting. Though I knew the war was bad I assumed a lot of it was your problem with alcohol. I never imagined the horrors and atrocities that you carried with you every day. The critics and veterans claim the movie to be a very accurate depiction, but always add, "You had to be there." Well, you were there,

Dad, and I am sorry to the point of being sick, but yet so proud that you pulled through.

As the soldiers were yelling into the radios that the first wave was ineffective, I recalled you telling how your wave, the fifth, was one of the first waves where anyone survived. I remember the young, red-haired boy that ran from the bombed-out building yelling "Comrade, comrade," only to be gunned down before you could save him. I know you walked for days with blistered feet in pouring rains to the beat of freedom's drums to help eliminate the evil that existed in that part of the world. All this, and on your death bed I couldn't forgive you for the struggles we shared.

The end of the movie shows Private Ryan as an older man, standing in the cemetery at the Omaha Beach Memorial in Normandy. He mutters that he hopes he has been the man that his commanding officer told him to be. He turns to his wife and says, "I am a good person, aren't I?" sharing a lifetime of doubts, guilt, and fears.

How many times in your drunkenness did you ask the same question and how many times in my life have I had the same thoughts about myself. We were both casualties of that awful war, but somehow, through determination or just plain stubbornness, we made it. I'm proud of you and I know you would be proud of me.

With love and respect,

Your son, Philip

I share the thoughts and stories of my life with you. I hope that they will help you understand your own spirit.

Your spirit is meant to be here at this time. Listen to that spirit as it walks through creation. Look at its weakness and create strengths from them. Look at its strengths and become humble. Never allow anyone, including yourself, to rob you of the spirit within yourself. Take time to love and nurture that spirit and be who God wants you to be. Learn to share in the love of your spirit and share your spirit in love.

Some of the things I share are wounds yet unhealed. Some are wounds that are healed but have left scars. Some are just wonderful memories that make my life what it is. I have come to understand the difference between love and hate. I have come to accept the differences in people and the role of human nature in the world in which we live. I have come to understand the presence of fear and the power of love. I know my faults although I often choose to deny them. I am still on my journey, seeking love and happiness. There have been people along the pathway that have been an integral part of that journey. Some have known of that love and some have denied it. Each day I pray that I can go through this day as honest as I allow myself to be. I pray that with honesty I can touch the true nature of the God within.

I do not expect life to always be a paradise, but I am prepared to handle the most difficult moments and have discovered that life itself has taught me to do so. As a person whose life was marred by addiction and abuse, I have come to realize that we can rise above or we can wallow in our own self-pity. I have recognized special gifts and talents within myself and have mingled those gifts with academic knowledge, spiritual belief, and an understanding of the human spirit, so that each day, no matter what happens . . . "I knew this day would come."